Garnishes
and decorations

Garnishes
and decorations

JANET BRINKWORTH

LORENZ BOOKS

For Mum and Dad, with love and thanks.

Published by Lorenz Books
an imprint of
Anness Publishing Limited
Hermes House, 88-89 Blackfriars Road
London SE1 8HA

This edition distributed in Canada by Raincoast Books
8680 Cambie Street, Vancouver, British Columbia V6P 6M9

ISBN 0-7548-0120-9

A CIP catalogue record for this book
is available from the British Library

Publisher: Joanna Lorenz
Senior Cookery Editor: Linda Fraser
Cookery Editor: Maggie Mayhew
Copy Editor: Jenni Fleetwood
Designer: Lilian Lindblom
Jacket Design: D.W. Design
Photography: Karl Adamson
Assistant Home Economist: Zoe Kean
Stylist: Clare Hunt

Previously published as part of the *Step-by-Step* cookery series

Printed and bound in China

© Anness Publishing Limited 1996, 1999
1 3 5 7 9 10 8 6 4 2

MEASUREMENTS
For all recipes, quantities are given in both metric and imperial measures, and,
where appropriate, measures are also given in standard cups and spoons. Follow
one set, but not a mixture, because they are not interchangeable.

CONTENTS

INTRODUCTION

Garnishing is probably the best way of transforming any recipe from
the ordinary to the extraordinary, using the simplest ingredients with
just a touch of effort and imagination. For example, take a simple dish of
grilled chicken, add a few sprigs of thyme and several olives, and it is
immediately transformed into a magical Mediterranean meal!

All sorts of ingredients can be used to garnish or decorate food – it is
often a good idea to echo the main ingredients of the dish, but a colourful
contrast can be just as effective. Opt for a classic, understated garnish,
designed to subtly embellish the dish, or a gloriously over-the-top item such
as red chillies tied together with raffia – a feast for the eye, not the palate.
Garnishes are fun as well as functional and provide a marvellous opportuni-
ty for stamping your own personality on the food you serve.

Vegetables, herbs, fruit and flowers, whether real or craftily sculpted to
imitate the original, may be used for garnishing. Chives are a favourite herb,
thanks to their versatility. Not only can they be chopped or sliced
but they can also be used as edible string for tying up bundles
of herbs or vegetables.

Presentation is as important as preparation. Choose your crockery with care,
selecting colours that enhance the food rather than clash with it. Avoid
overpowering patterns unless the food is very plain. You don't have to be an
accomplished artist to excel at garnishing. Some of the simplest effects can
be stunning. Experiment to find the most pleasing arrangement, whether this
is an elaborate decoration around the rim of a dish or merely a few carefully
chosen garden flowers laid on top of a cake.

Equipment

It is not necessary to have a vast array of equipment or gadgets for making garnishes, but there are some items that will make the task infinitely easier.

Cannelle knife

This tool is great for carving stripes in the skin of citrus fruit. It is also good for decorating cucumbers, courgettes or any other soft-skinned vegetables. Pare off thin strips before slicing the fruit or vegetable, to make an attractive edge.

Cutters

A basic set of round cutters can be expanded gradually to include diamonds, squares, stars, hearts and flowers. Use them to cut out shapes from thinly sliced vegetables, or slivers of red and green pepper or citrus peel. Look out for tiny aspic cutters in a variety of interesting shapes.

Knives

A small turning, or paring, knife is essential for carving out designs on fruit skins, such as melon, and also for fluting button mushrooms. A good sharp cook's knife or chopping knife will make chopping herbs a simple job. Make sure you regularly sharpen knives to maintain the blades.

Melon baller

A handy little tool with either a large or small scoop, this is used to make small balls of fruit or vegetables.

Pastry brushes

Buy good-quality brushes with tightly packed bristles. A normal paintbrush can be used, as long as the bristles are securely fixed, it is washed thoroughly before use and, of course, isn't used for painting!

Piping bags and nozzles

A medium piping bag with a selection of nozzles is very useful to have for garnishing sweet and savoury dishes. Use small disposable piping bags for chocolate or icing, where a fine line is required.

Raffia

An excellent standby for tying almost anything, raffia looks much more attractive than string. It is now available in all sorts of colours and can be bought in most florists or good garden centres.

Ribbon

Keep a small stock in various colours and widths for that final finishing touch. Use ribbon to tie round cold soufflé or mousse dishes or tie round garlands of fresh flowers or leaves to keep them in place.

Sieves

Both large and small sieves are essential items in any kitchen.

Skewers and cocktail sticks

Wooden and metal skewers can be used in a variety of ways, as can cocktail sticks. Drop spots of cream on to fruit sauces and use the point of a cocktail stick or skewer to drag the spots into heart or star shapes.

Small scissors

These are perfect for small garnishes where knives would be difficult to use. They are especially useful for snipping chives and other herbs.

Swivel-blade peelers

Both long-handled and broad-handled peelers can be used for much more than just peeling potatoes and carrots. Use to pare vegetables into thin strips before cooking.

Tea strainer

A tea strainer will come in handy for sifting icing sugar over small items such as individual mousses and single servings of desserts.

Zester

Ideal for cucumbers and citrus fruit, a zester has the same function as a cannelle knife but produces a row of thin stripes.

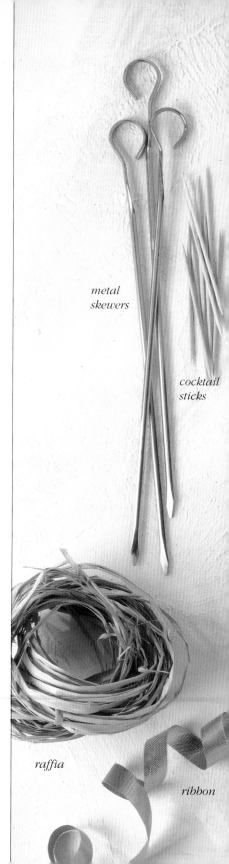

metal skewers

cocktail sticks

raffia

ribbon

wooden skewers

sieve

swivel-blade peelers

cannelle knife

zester

melon baller

tea strainer

cutters

scissors

knives

piping bags and nozzles

pastry brushes

Store Cupboard Standbys

A surprising number of garnishes can be made in advance and stored, ready for use later. Keep these items handy in a pantry or fridge and you should never have a problem in providing an instant garnish.

Biscuits

Sweet and savoury biscuits can be made ahead of time. Simply cut into shapes, bake and then store in airtight tins or freeze them. To use, thaw for half an hour, dust sweet biscuits with icing sugar and serve with mousses and fruit fools.

Chive braids

These can be made 1–2 days ahead and kept on damp kitchen paper in an airtight box in the fridge.

Chocolate curls and leaves

These can be made up to a month in advance and stored in a cool place on greaseproof paper in airtight containers.

Cinnamon sticks

Tie together long cinnamon sticks, using ribbon or raffia and store them in an airtight container. Place the tied bundles at the side of serving plates for an unusual touch.

Cucumbers

Keep a piece of cucumber in the crisper drawer of your fridge and you'll find that you can always use it to rustle up a garnish in a matter of minutes.

Dried chillies

Large and small dried chillies look stunning in a bowl in the kitchen and are then readily available to use as a garnish tied together with a little raffia.

Fresh chillies

Bright red and green chillies make an attractive addition to Oriental dishes. Use raffia to tie together bunches of chillies; add one or two sprigs of fresh herbs, if you like.

Fruit purées

Made in advance and frozen in ice cube trays, these are marvellous for decorating desserts. Thaw the cubes of frozen fruit purée in the microwave or in a saucepan, swirl on a plate and top with the dessert.

Herb butter

Rolls of herb butter can be frozen, ready for slicing at a moment's notice. Serve on top of grilled meat, poultry or fish.

Herbs

The best herbs are home-grown, but purchased herbs will stay fresh in the fridge for 4–5 days. Trim off the ends, wash and shake well, then place on damp kitchen paper in a storage box.

Lemons and limes

These fruits keep well and with a few simple cuts can quickly be transformed into a variety of garnishes. They can be used for both sweet and savoury dishes.

Oranges

These can be cut into wedges or slices and the slices can then be turned into a cone or a twist, for a very colourful, edible garnish or decoration.

Parmesan cheese

Nothing lifts a plate of pasta more than a delicate curl of Parmesan, and a salad becomes special when topped with a few Parmesan shavings.

Radishes

Cut into roses using a small sharp knife or make zig-zag cuts around the middle and pull apart to make Vandyke radishes. Radishes can also be left whole, with their leaves attached, to garnish a salad.

Redcurrant bunches

Drape bunches of redcurrants over sweet dishes, or tie two together with long pieces of fresh chives.

raffia

fresh flowers

chocolate

oranges

herbs

radishes

fresh
chillies

dried chillies

lemons and
limes

Parmesan
cheese

cucumbers

cinnamon sticks

redcurrant
bunches

Easy Ways with Herbs

Forget the forlorn sprig of parsley: herbs can be used in a huge variety of ways. They can be chopped, sliced, used in strands or bound in a bouquet. Here are some speedy suggestions.

Basil
A cluster of leaves looks and tastes marvellous on tomatoes. Alternatively, scatter single leaves over salads and pizzas.

Bay
The leaves from this attractive evergreen tree can be used all year to garnish roast meat, poultry and any recipe that uses bay in it. The glossy leaves can be used singly or in small sprigs.

Carrot tops
Not strictly a herb, carrot tops can be used in much the same way. Young carrot tops make an unusual garnish for platters: rinse, shake dry, then lay alongside the food.

Chives
Chives can be prepared in a variety of ways:
• Finely chopped – chop or snip them into tiny pieces.
• Coarsely chopped – cut to a length of about 5 mm/¼ in.
• Cut on the diagonal – chop them any length you like, these look especially good on Oriental dishes.
• Wilted – place them on kitchen paper on a plate in the microwave. Heat for 3–5 seconds on High. Refresh under cold water, and pat dry. Use as an edible tie or braid.

Coriander
Fresh sprigs of coriander are a must when making Oriental or Eastern food. Coriander can be coarsely chopped and sprinkled over all sorts of savoury Indian and Asian dishes for an unbeatable flavour.

Dill
Dill looks great when it is snipped into fronds and sprinkled over food. It also chops well, giving a lighter effect than either parsley or chives. Use sprigs of fresh dill with a twist of fresh lemon to garnish fish dishes.

Fennel
The delicate green leaves from the fennel plant look very similar to fresh dill. It can be used in the same way as dill and imparts an aniseed flavour that is particularly good with fish or in Mediterranean dishes.

Mixed herbs
All herbs look good with a simple lemon or cucumber slice or twist. Just place a herb sprig so that it pokes out from under the slice. Form small bunches of herbs into a bouquet – take a small handful and twist off the stems, then carefully tease the leaves out using a cocktail stick.

Parsley
Both flat leaf and curly parsley have their uses. A small sprig of flat leaf parsley looks more appealing than one of curly, yet when curly parsley is finely chopped it looks great scattered over rice or potatoes.

Sage
Sage has a wonderful texture and colour that adds interest to herb bouquets. It can be used on its own to garnish pork or poultry dishes. Purple sage is particularly stunning and can be used to great effect.

Scented geranium
The serrated leaves of the scented geranium make an attractive decoration for sorbets and ice creams. Use it in place of mint sprigs for an unusual, beautiful bouquet.

Watercress
Use watercress to garnish plates of sandwiches and fish, poultry and beef dishes. Gather together several fresh sprigs, twist off the bottoms of the stalks and place on the side of large serving dishes.

chopped parsley

flat leaf parsley

carrot tops

basil

watercress

chopped
dill

chives

dill sprig and
lemon twist

sage

dill

carrot batons

Simple Vegetable Garnishes

The vegetable most often used for garnishing is the cucumber. It can be cut and sliced in a wide variety of ways, some of which are described below, together with suggestions for using peppers, leeks, tomatoes and French beans.

Cucumber
• Spirals – cut two slices, each 3 mm/⅛ in thick. Make a cut from the centre to the edge on both slices. Twist each slice into an "S" shape. Place the spirals next to each other and link them together.
• Border – cut six slices, each 3 mm/⅛ in thick, then cut each slice in half. Place around the rim of the plate, arranging alternate slices skin-side inwards and skin-side outwards.
• Fan – cut a cucumber into 5 cm/2 in lengths. Then cut each piece in half lengthways. Make six or seven very fine cuts three-quarters of the way into the cucumber half. Press down gently and fan out the slices.

French beans
Slice beans at an angle into 2 cm/¾ in lengths. Scatter over salads or use in pairs to make a cross on top of a canapé.

Leek curls
Cut a leek into 5 cm/2 in lengths, then slice in half lengthways. Cut the leek strips into fine matchsticks. Put them in a bowl of iced water and chill for 2 hours or until they form tight curls. Drain the curls before using.

Mushrooms
Use a small sharp knife to cut small grooves in a spiral around the caps of button mushrooms, Use these "turned" mushrooms raw or lightly cook in butter until golden. Place a few on each diner's plate to thrill and impress your guests.

Pepper triangles
Cut 1 red and 1 yellow pepper into quarters, remove the seeds, then cut out 2 x 1 cm/¾ x ½ in rectangles. Make a cut two-thirds of the way into the short side, three-quarters of the way up. Turn the piece of pepper 180° and repeat. Twist the pepper and pull to form a triangle. Alternate the red and yellow triangles around the rim of a plate, as a border, or use just one or two as a garnish for individual servings.

Radishes
Make zig-zag cuts around the middle and pull apart to make Vandyke radishes. Use with the fresh green leaves still intact, to brighten up salads and other cold dishes.

Spring onions
Use a small sharp knife to cut the green ends of spring onions into fine long shreds that are still attached to the white part. Plunge the spring onions into iced water and leave overnight to allow the ends to curl up. This can also be done with shorter lengths of shredded spring onion. Use these curly shreds to scatter over salads and hot savoury dishes.

Tomato bowl
Using a small sharp knife cut a "V" into the middle of a large firm tomato, inserting the knife right through to the centre. Make identical cuts all the way round the tomato so that it looks as though a zig-zag line has been drawn around it. Gently pull the tomato apart and top each half with two quarter slices of cucumber and a parsley sprig.

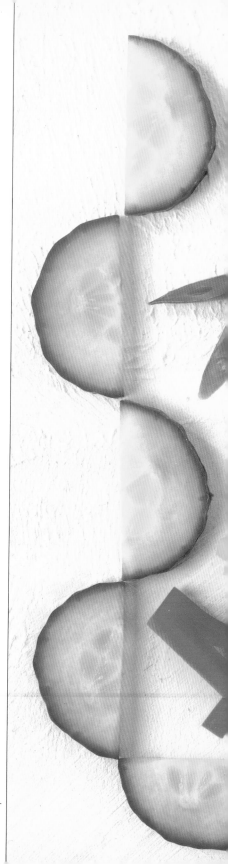

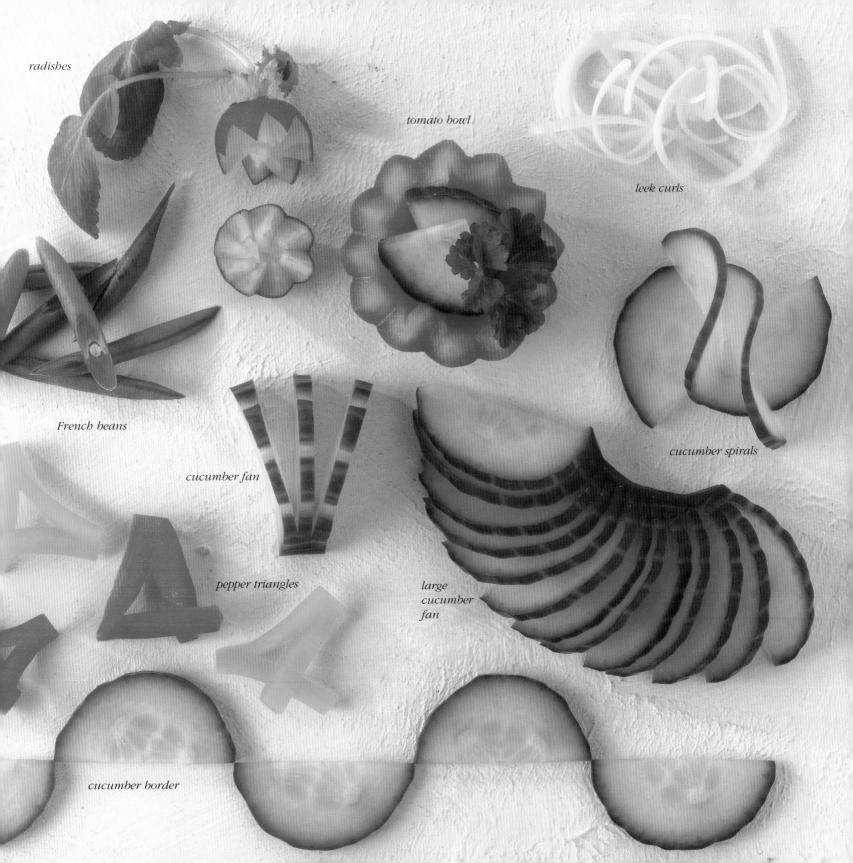

radishes

tomato bowl

leek curls

French beans

cucumber fan

cucumber spirals

pepper triangles

large
cucumber
fan

cucumber border

Using Fruit and Flowers

Some of the most eye-catching garnishes and decorations are made from fruit and flowers.

Baby rose posy

Choose six perfect small roses and trim the stems to about 2.5 cm/1 in. Place five of the roses in a ring on a cake so that the stems meet in the centre. Place the remaining rose on top to finish the posy.

Edible flowers

Edible flowers, such as nasturtiums, can be used to enliven a salad or a scoop of ice cream. Simply scatter several across the plate. Both blue and white borage flowers look stunning in salads and drinks during the summer months.

Flower bouquet

Gather some fresh flowers together in a bouquet, tie with some raffia or a ribbon and place on top of a cake.

Lemon basket

Holding a lemon lengthways, cut it in half around the middle to within 5 mm/¼ in of the centre. Make an identical cut on the opposite side of the lemon. Slice down from the top to meet the first incision, then make a similar cut from the top to the second incision. Pull the loose segments away and discard. Cut out the flesh under the "handle" and discard it. Put a sprig of dill in the centre of the lemon basket and place on a dish of canapés or use to garnish a large, whole, cooked fish.

Lemon wedges

Cut a lemon lengthways in half, then cut each half into three wedges. Carefully remove any pips. Arrange the wedges on the plate in pairs, separated by a sprig of parsley. Use a lime instead, if you prefer.

Lime segments

Peel a lime, making sure that you remove all the pith. Separate into neat segments, cutting between each of the membranes. Place the segments in pairs, and arrange a little salad cress on top.

Melon bowl

Insert a small sharp knife halfway down a cantaloupe melon at an angle and push it in as far as the centre. Cut a series of deep "V" shapes all the way around the melon until you get back to where you started. Gently pull the melon apart and remove the seeds from both halves. Using a melon baller, scoop the flesh of one half into small balls and place these in the cavity of the other half.

Orange flower

Cut two thin slices from an orange, then cut each slice in half. Cut along the inside of the pith on one half to within 3 mm/⅛ in of the end. Turn the strip of rind in, to form a loop on top of the half slice. Repeat with the remaining half slices. Place them in a ring with the loops on the outside.

Pear fan

Peel a pear, leaving the stem intact. Poach in a light syrup until tender. Cut in half lengthways. Place cut-side down on a chopping board and cut about eight thin slices, leaving then intact at the top. Press down gently to fan the slices apart.

Strawberry fan

Make a strawberry into a fan by cutting into thin slices, from the pointed end, almost to the top. Leave the strawberry hull and calyx in place and gently fan out the strawberry slices. Make half strawberry fans by halving the strawberry first and then placing the cut side down on a board. Make cuts from the leaf end almost to the pointed end and fan out gently.

lemon basket

lemon wedges

lime segments

fresh flowers

orange flower

flower bouquet

pear fan

strawberry
fan

baby rose
posy

melon bowl

TECHNIQUES

Preparing ingredients is easy when you follow
these step-by-step instructions.

Cutting Carrot Julienne

It may seem a little time-consuming and fiddly
to cut vegetables into thin julienne strips, but the
result is definitely worth it.

1 Peel a carrot and take a thin slice off each side to square it up. Cut into
5 cm/2 in lengths.

2 Cut each of the lengths into
5 mm/¼ in thick slices.

3 Stack the slices and cut these into
fine matchsticks to form julienne.

Making a Radish Rose

This is a classic garnish. The technique can also
be applied to the bulb of a salad onion or a baby
turnip. Radish roses can be made in advance and
kept in water in the fridge for up to 3 days.

1 Carefully trim both ends of the
radish, removing the root and stalk.

2 Place base-end down and cut in
half vertically, stopping the knife just
before it reaches the base. Repeat until
the radish looks as though it has been
cut into eight equal segments, but is in
fact held together at the base.

3 Put the radish in a bowl of iced water and leave for at least 4 hours to open up.

Blanching

Blanching is a method of partial cooking, where foods are immersed in boiling water or boiled briefly. In terms of garnishing, the technique is used to make vegetables, fruit or herbs more pliable and easier to handle. It also helps to preserve a bright colour.

1 Fill a large saucepan with water and bring to the boil. Add the prepared vegetable or fruit for the time suggested in each individual recipe: 1–2 minutes is usually ample.

2 Drain well in a colander, then refresh in cold water. Change the water once or twice, as necessary, until the food is completely cold. Drain again.

3 Blanched vegetables and fruit can be used in various ways: stamped out into diamonds, perhaps, or tied in a bundle with a wilted chive.

Peeling Tomatoes

It only takes a few moments to peel tomatoes, but the difference this makes to a dish is amazing. Concassing tomatoes (chopping them into neat squares) adds the finishing touch.

1 Make a small cross in the skin on the base of each tomato. Use a small sharp knife to cut out the calyx.

2 Place the tomatoes in boiling water for 20–30 seconds, drain and refresh under cold water. Gently peel off the loosened skin.

3 Cut the tomatoes into quarters. Place each tomato quarter flesh-side down and slide a knife along the inner flesh, scooping out all the seeds. Cut the flesh into neat 5 mm/¼ in squares.

Piping

Piping is an art that anyone can master with a bit of practice. It is widely used as a form of decoration, for shaping biscuits, creating a decorative border with mashed potato or making attractively shaped meringues.

1 Select the right nozzle – a star for a rosette, for instance, or a small plain nozzle for writing. Half-fill the piping bag, then twist it closed, at the same time expelling any air.

2 Hold the bag firmly in one hand, with your fingers around the twisted section. Use the other hand to lightly guide the nozzle. Exert a very firm, steady pressure and start to pipe. The trick is to keep the pressure steady until the design is finished. A sudden squeeze will produce a large blob rather than an even flow.

3 As soon as the design is complete, stop applying pressure, push down slightly and quickly lift up the nozzle.

Melting Chocolate

Melting chocolate takes a little patience and care, but the process is very simple. It can be done over hot water or in a microwave oven.

1 To microwave, break 115 g/4 oz plain chocolate into squares or chop it into small pieces. Place in a heatproof bowl and cook on medium (50% power) for 2 minutes. Milk and white chocolate should be melted for the same time, but on low (30% power).

2 To melt chocolate over hot water, bring a small saucepan of water to the boil. Turn off the heat and place the bowl of chocolate over the hot water. The bowl must not touch the water nor should any drops of water be allowed to fall into the chocolate or it will become grainy.

3 Leave the chocolate until very soft, then stir it lightly. Melted chocolate can be used in many ways: spooned into paper piping bags and piped, drizzled over tiny cup cakes or mixed with a little cream and spread over a cake as an icing.

Frosting

Frosting is a classic decoration, usually used for fruit or flowers. Try arranging frosted grapes on a cheesecake, or scatter frosted rose petals around a delicate lemon mousse. Whole roses can also be decorated in this way.

1 Separate the petals of a rose or cut grapes into small bunches. Whisk an egg white until it starts to become foamy. Brush gently on to each of the rose petals or grapes, covering them completely.

2 Sprinkle caster sugar on to a sheet of greaseproof paper. Place the rose petals or grapes on the sheet and sprinkle over more sugar, then toss lightly until completely covered.

3 Place the rose petals or grapes on a wire rack and leave for several hours until completey dry.

Stencilling

Stencilling can be a fun way to liven up sponge cakes, biscuits or even a soufflé! There are no hard and fast rules – experiment with different templates such as lacy paper doilys.

1 Place a cake on a sheet of grease-proof paper. Cut out strips of paper and lay these in a random criss-cross pattern across the cake. Dust with icing sugar, then carefully remove the paper strips to reveal the pattern.

2 For a two-tone effect, dust a cake with icing sugar, covering it completely. Place a doily lightly over the cake and dust with cocoa. Lift off carefully.

3 Cut a small design or initial out of card and place it over a biscuit. Dust the biscuit with icing sugar or cocoa before carefully removing the card.

Petal Sushi with Chilli Flowers

Make these chilli flowers several hours before needed to allow the "flowers" to open up fully.

Makes 24

INGREDIENTS
45 ml/3 tbsp rice wine vinegar
10 ml/2 tsp caster sugar
2.5 ml/½ tsp salt
225 g/8 oz/1¼ cups Thai fragrant rice, cooked and still warm
4–8 asparagus spears, trimmed
15 ml/1 tbsp wasabi (hot green horseradish)
20 g/¾ oz/1 tbsp pickled ginger, thinly sliced
4 toasted nori sheets
4 red chillies, to garnish

wasabi

rice wine

red chillies

Thai fragrant rice

asparagus spears

toasted nori

caster sugar

COOK'S TIP
Wear rubber gloves or wash your hands thoroughly after handling chillies as they can irritate the skin severely.

1 Start by making the garnish. Use a small pair of scissors or a slim-bladed knife to cut a chilli carefully lengthways up from the tip to within 1 cm/½ in of the stem end. Repeat this at regular intervals around the chilli – more cuts will produce more petals. Repeat with the remaining chillies.

2 Rinse the chillies in cold water and remove all the seeds. Place the chillies in a bowl of iced water and chill for at least 4 hours. For very curly flowers, leave the chillies overnight.

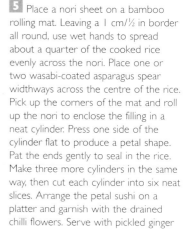

3 Place the rice wine vinegar, sugar and salt in a small saucepan and heat gently until the sugar has dissolved. Pour the rice wine mixture over the rice and fold in, using a cutting action to mix evenly. Allow the mixture to cool.

4 Cook the asparagus in boiling water until just tender. Drain, refresh in cold water and pat dry. Spread a little wasabi over each asparagus spear until thinly coated. Fold the pickled ginger slices around the asparagus.

5 Place a nori sheet on a bamboo rolling mat. Leaving a 1 cm/½ in border all round, use wet hands to spread about a quarter of the cooked rice evenly across the nori. Place one or two wasabi-coated asparagus spear widthways across the centre of the rice. Pick up the corners of the mat and roll up the nori to enclose the filling in a neat cylinder. Press one side of the cylinder flat to produce a petal shape. Pat the ends gently to seal in the rice. Make three more cylinders in the same way, then cut each cylinder into six neat slices. Arrange the petal sushi on a platter and garnish with the drained chilli flowers. Serve with pickled ginger and a chilli dipping sauce.

Wild Rice Blinis with Vegetable Shreds

The vegetable shreds – baby julienne strips – can be arranged to form little haystacks on each blini or piled higgledy-piggledy; either way you'll find it produces a stunning result.

Makes 40

INGREDIENTS
165 g/5½ oz/scant 1½ cups
 wholemeal flour
300 ml/½ pint/1¼ cups
 soured cream
115 g/4 oz/½ cup wild rice
2 eggs, beaten
25 g/1 oz/2 tbsp butter, melted
5 ml/1 tsp baking powder
10 ml/2 tsp bicarbonate of soda
15 ml/1 tbsp hot water
oil, for frying
salt and freshly ground black
 pepper
250 ml/8fl oz/1 cup crème
 fraîche, to serve

FOR THE GARNISH
1 each red, yellow and green
 peppers, seeded and quartered
1 carrot, peeled
½ cucumber

1 Put the flour in a bowl. Gradually add the soured cream, mixing until smooth. Cover and chill for at least 2 hours. Meanwhile, boil the wild rice in plenty of water for 45–50 minutes until slightly overcooked. Drain, rinse under cold water, then drain again. Set aside.

2 Make the garnish. Cut the red and yelow peppers, the carrot and the cucumber into julienne strips 2 cm/¾ in long and 5 mm/¼ in wide. Cover and chill until they are required.

3 Preheat the oven to 140°C/275°F/Gas 1. Line a baking sheet with greaseproof paper. Beat the eggs, butter and baking powder into the flour mixture. Mix the bicarbonate of soda with the hot water and stir into the batter with the rice.

4 Add a little salt and pepper to the batter. Heat a little oil in a heavy-based frying pan, then drop in small spoonfuls of the rice batter. Cook until bubbles appear on the surface of each blini and they become firm. Flip the blinis over and cook the other side briefly. Stack on the prepared baking sheet and keep warm in the oven. Repeat with the remaining batter. Serve the blinis warm, topped with crème fraîche. Garnish each blini with the vegetable shreds.

oil

soured cream

butter

baking powder

wild rice

crème fraîche

wholemeal flour

eggs

bicarbonate of soda

carrot

red and yellow peppers

cucumber

Chilli Prawns in Cucumber Cups on a Herb-rimmed Plate

Try garnishing the rim of the plate rather than the food itself – a very simple but stunning idea.

Makes 20– 24

INGREDIENTS
4 small red chillies, seeded and
  finely diced
10 ml/2 tsp finely grated fresh
  root ginger
1 large garlic clove, crushed
45 ml/3 tbsp light soy sauce
225 g/8 oz cooked prawns,
  peeled and deveined
2 cucumbers

FOR THE GARNISH
15 g/½ oz/1 tbsp butter,
  softened
30 ml/2 tbsp chopped fresh
  chives

prawns

chives   garlic

butter   red chillies

cucumber

soy sauce   root
                 ginger

COOK'S TIP
Use any type of chopped herb
or, for a more colourful edge,
dust with chilli powder or
ground turmeric.

1 Combine the chillies, ginger, garlic
and soy sauce in a bowl. Add the
prawns and toss them in the marinade.
Cover and chill for 2– 4 hours.

2 Trim both ends of the cucumbers,
then cut them into 2 cm/¾ in lengths.
Use a 3 cm/1¼ in round aspic cutter to
stamp out rounds and discard the skin.

3 Using a melon baller, scoop out the
cucumber seeds to make little cups.
Place upside-down on kitchen paper to
drain for 20–30 minutes.

4 Brush the butter around the rim of
the plate. Sprinkle the chives over the
butter to form a decorative edge. Tip
the plate and shake lightly to remove
any loose chives. Arrange the cucumber
cups in the centre of the plate and fill
each one with 2–3 marinated prawns.

Poppadums with Caviar and Chopped Egg

An unusual way of serving caviar – topped with a garnish of chopped hard-boiled egg.

Makes 24

INGREDIENTS
6 ready-to-cook poppadums
25 g/1 oz caviar or black lumpfish roe
2 hard-boiled eggs, to garnish

poppadums

caviar   *eggs*

 1 Preheat the grill to high. Cut the poppadums carefully into quarters, using a pair of kitchen scissors.

2 Place several poppadum quarters on a foil-lined grill tray. Watching all the time, grill for 5–10 seconds or until they have turned white and have curled up. Remove, then repeat with the remaining poppadums. Store in an airtight container for up to 3 days.

3 Shell the eggs and cut them in half. Scoop the yolks into a sieve and set aside. Chop the whites very finely.

4 Using the back of a spoon, rub the reserved egg yolk through the sieve into a small bowl. Place a small spoonful of caviar or lumpfish roe on one corner of each poppadum. Top with a small amount of egg white and a tiny dot of egg yolk. Serve at once.

Baby Ginger Rösti with Chilli Bouquets

Chillies make a wonderfully versatile garnish – even a single chilli placed on the side of a plate can set off a dish.

Makes 20–24

INGREDIENTS
450 g/1 lb potatoes
30 ml/2 tbsp grated fresh
    root ginger
15 ml/1 tbsp plain flour
oil, for frying
salt and freshly ground black
    pepper

FOR THE GARNISH
2 large red chillies
raffia, for tying
large sprigs of parsley or
    coriander (optional)

raffia

potatoes

plain flour

oil

red chillies

root ginger

parsley

1 Preheat the oven to 140°C/275°F/ Gas 1. Line a baking sheet with kitchen paper. Peel the potatoes and grate them coarsely into a bowl. Stir in the ginger. Add the flour, salt and pepper, then mix together well.

3 Fry the rösti for 2–3 minutes on each side until golden brown.

2 Heat a little oil in a non-stick frying pan, then gently drop in a few small spoonfuls of the coarsely grated potato mixture.

4 Place on the prepared baking sheet and keep warm in the oven. Make more rösti in the same way.

5 To make the garnish, simply tie the stems of the chillies together with a small piece of raffia. For an interesting colour contrast add a large parsley or coriander sprig. Arrange the rösti on a plate, set the chillies on the rim and serve at once.

Smoked Mackerel Pâté with Lemon Twists

Linking several lemon twists together with a sprig of parsley creates a simple but effective result.

Makes 40 – 50

INGREDIENTS
12 slices Granary bread
250 g/9 oz smoked
 mackerel fillets, skinned
115 g/4 oz/½ cup cream cheese
90 g/3½ oz/½ cup Greek yogurt
25 ml/5 tsp horseradish cream
5 ml/1 tsp paprika

FOR THE GARNISH
1 lemon
sprig of parsley

parsley

cream cheese

Greek yogurt

smoked mackerel fillets

horseradish cream

paprika

Granary bread

lemon

1 Preheat the oven to 150°C/300°F/ Gas 2. Using a small round cutter stamp out rounds of bread.

2 Place on a baking sheet and place in the oven. Bake for 30 – 40 minutes until hard and lightly golden. Place on a rack to cool. These can be made in advance and stored in an airtight tin for up to a week.

3 Place the smoked mackerel, cream cheese, yogurt and horseradish into a food processor. Process until smooth.

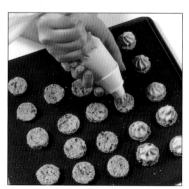

4 Place the pâté in a piping bag fitted wth a star nozzle and pipe a small rosette on to each toast. Dust each one with a little paprika.

5 To make the garnish, use a sharp knife to cut the lemon into 5 mm/¼ in slices. Make a cut in each slice from the centre out to the skin.

6 Hold the slice either side of the cut and twist to form an "S" shape. Place three together and place a sprig of parsley under one end slice.

Pear and Stilton Grills with a Gilded Pear

Gilding is a stunning way to finish a dish. Any fruit can be transformed like this and even used as an unusual table decoration.

Makes 24

INGREDIENTS
4 large ripe eating pears
115 g/4 oz/1 cup Stilton cheese
30 ml/2 tbsp Greek yogurt
salt and freshly ground black
  pepper

FOR THE GARNISH
1 small pear, preferably
  with stalk intact
1 book of edible gold leaf

pears

Stilton cheese

edible gold leaf

Greek yogurt

1 Make the garnish. Stand the small pear upright. If the base is particularly rounded, you may find it necessary to trim about 5 mm/¼ in off the base of the pear so that it remains level.

2 Tear off pieces of gold leaf and press over the pear, smoothing the leaf on carefully until the pear is covered evenly. Set aside.

3 Preheat the grill to high. Line a grill pan with foil. Cut the large pears lengthways into thick slices on either side of the core. Using a small diamond aspic cutter, stamp out about 24 diamonds of pear and place in the prepared grill pan.

4 Crumble the Stilton into a bowl. Stir in the yogurt to make a creamy paste, then add salt and pepper to taste. Place a teaspoonful of the mixture on each pear diamond. Grill until the Stilton starts to melt and bubble. Arrange on a platter with the gilded pear and serve immediately.

Egg and Tomato Tartlets with a Quail's Egg Nest

Quail's eggs make a delightful garnish with their pretty shells left on. Hard-boil some and use as an edible garnish, but shell before eating.

Makes 24

INGREDIENTS
24 cooked tartlet cases
24 quail's eggs
6 cherry tomatoes
24 parsley sprigs
salt and freshly ground
  black pepper

FOR THE GARNISH
12 quail's eggs
2 leeks, trimmed

quail's eggs

cherry tomatoes

tartlet cases

leek

parsley

1 Preheat the oven to 180°C/350°F/Gas 4. Season the tartlet cases and place them on baking sheets. Carefully break the quail's eggs into a bowl, taking care to keep the yolks intact. Cut the cherry tomatoes into quarters.

2 Spoon a yolk into each tartlet. Add a small amount of egg white to each, but do not overfill. Place a tomato quarter in each tartlet. Cover with foil and bake for 10–12 minutes until just set. Top each one with a parsley sprig.

3 Make the garnish. Place the quail's eggs in a saucepan of cold water, bring to the boil, cover and remove from the heat. Leave for 6–8 minutes. Drain the eggs and refresh under cold running water until they are cool. Drain and pat the shells dry.

4 Shred the leeks finely by hand or by using a food processor fitted with a fine shredding plate. Form the shredded leeks into a nest on a large platter, with the hard-boiled quail's eggs nestled on top. Add the warm egg and tomato tartlets and serve.

Potato Blinis with Dill Cream and Smoked Salmon Roses

A rose of smoked salmon complements fluffy potato blinis perfectly and provides a very interesting combination of flavours and textures.

Serves 8

INGREDIENTS
450 g/1 lb floury potatoes,
   peeled and quartered
3 eggs, beaten
60 ml/4 tbsp self-raising flour
150 ml/¼ pint/⅔ cup double
   cream
2 egg whites
5 ml/1 tsp grated nutmeg
oil, for frying
salt and freshly ground black
   pepper
60 ml/4 tbsp dill mustard and
   300 ml/½ pint/1¼ cups crème
   fraîche, to serve

TO GARNISH
8 smoked salmon slices
sprigs of dill

smoked salmon   *double cream*   *potatoes*   *nutmeg*   *dill mustard*   *eggs*   *crème fraîche*   *self-raising flour*

1 Cook the potatoes in boiling lightly salted water until tender. Drain, return to the saucepan and place over a low heat to steam dry and drive off any excess moisture. Pass through a food mill (or press through a sieve with a wooden spoon) into a bowl. Mash lightly, then cool, cover and chill. Mix the dill mustard and crème fraîche in a bowl, cover and set aside.

2 Whisk the eggs and flour into the chilled mashed potatoes. Bring the double cream to the boil in a small saucepan, then whisk into the potato mixture until it forms a batter. Whisk the egg whites in a grease-free bowl until stiff peaks form. Gently fold these into the potato batter. Season with nutmeg, salt and pepper, then set aside.

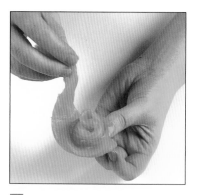

3 Make the garnish. Fold one slice of smoked salmon lengthways in half. Holding one end with finger and thumb, start rolling the salmon around on itself to form a loose pinwheel.

4 Set the salmon rose on the work surface and gently pinch the base to hold it together. Using a cocktail stick or small knife, gently separate each layer to form petals. Use the remaining smoked salmon to make more roses in the same way. Cover and chill.

5 Preheat the oven to 140°C/275°F/ Gas 1. Line a baking sheet with grease-proof paper. Heat a little oil in a small non-stick frying pan or crêpe pan. Ladle in about 1 cm/½ in batter. Cook until golden and bubbles have started to form on top. Flip over and cook the other side until golden.

6 Slide the blini on to the prepared baking sheet and keep warm in the oven. Make 7 more blinis in the same way, greasing the pan with a little oil each time. Serve the blinis warm, topping each one with a spoonful of dill cream and a smoked salmon rose. Garnish with sprigs of dill.

Thai Vichyssoise with Chive Braids

Give a classic French recipe an Oriental slant and serve it topped with edible braids of chives.

Serves 6

INGREDIENTS
50 g/2 oz/¼ cup butter
4 medium leeks, trimmed and
    thinly sliced
2 onions, thinly sliced
30 ml/2 tbsp Thai green
    curry paste
2 lime leaves
350 g/12 oz floury potatoes,
    peeled and diced
1 litre/1¾ pints/4 cups
    vegetable stock
2 x 400 ml/14 fl oz cans
    coconut milk
15 ml/1 tbsp fish sauce
30–60 thick chives, about
    20 cm/8 in long, to garnish

coconut milk

onion

fish sauce

butter

Thai green curry paste

leek

chives

potato

lime leaves

1 Melt the butter in a large saucepan. Add the leeks, onions, curry paste and lime leaves. Stir to mix, then cover and cook for 15 minutes until the onions are tender but not coloured.

2 Add the potatoes, stock and coconut milk. Bring to the boil, lower the heat, cover and simmer for about 25–30 minutes or until the potatoes are tender. Remove the lime leaves.

3 Purée the mixture in batches in a blender or pass through a food mill. Return to the clean pan and season with the fish sauce. Set aside.

4 Make the garnish. Pick out three of the thickest chives and two that are slightly thinner. Align the thicker chives on a work surface with a small bowl on one end to hold them still. Carefully plait the chives together to within 2.5 cm/1 in of the end.

5 Tie one of the thinner chives around the exposed end of the plait, then remove the bowl or board and tie the other end in the same way. Trim the ends of the ties and braids neatly with kitchen scissors. Make five to eleven more braids in the same way.

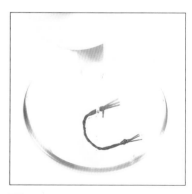

6 Place the braids in a bowl and pour boiling water over them. Leave to stand for 20–30 seconds then drain and refresh under cold water. Drain again. Reheat the soup or serve it chilled, with one or two of the chive braids floating on the top.

Prosciutto Salad with an Avocado Fan

Avocados are amazingly versatile – they can serve as edible containers, be sliced or diced in a salad, or form the foundation of a delicious soup or sauce. However, they are at their most elegant when sliced thinly and fanned on a plate.

Serves 4

INGREDIENTS
3 avocados
150 g/5 oz prosciutto
75–115 g/3–4 oz rocket
24 marinated black olives,
  drained

FOR THE DRESSING
15 ml/1 tbsp balsamic vinegar
5 ml/1 tsp lemon juice
5 ml/1 tsp prepared
  English mustard
5 ml/1 tsp sugar
75 ml/5 tbsp olive oil
salt and freshly ground black
  pepper

prosciutto

rocket

avocados

English mustard

olive oil

black olives

lemon

1 Make the dressing by combining the balsamic vinegar, lemon juice, mustard and sugar in a bowl. Whisk in the oil, season to taste, and set aside.

2 Cut 2 avocados in half. Remove the stones and skin, and cut into 1 cm/½ in slices. Toss with half the dressing. Place the prosciutto, avocado and rocket on four plates. Sprinkle the olives and the remaining dressing over the salads.

3 Make the garnish. Halve, stone and peel the remaining avocado. Slice each half lengthways into quarters. Gently draw a cannelle knife across the quarters at 1 cm/½ in intervals, to create regular stripes.

4 Make four cuts lengthways down each avocado quarter leaving 1 cm/½ in intact at the end. Carefully fan out the slices and arrange on the plate.

King Prawns with Salsa Verde and Lime Wedges

Limes are wonderfully versatile and look great simply cut into wedges, then dusted with a little finely chopped coriander or parsley.

Serves 4

INGREDIENTS
120 ml/4 fl oz/½ cup white
  wine
10 ml/2 tsp grated fresh
  root ginger
10 ml/2 tsp crushed garlic
24 raw king prawns, peeled
  and heads left intact
2 limes and 30 ml/1 tbsp
  chopped fresh coriander,
  to garnish

FOR THE SALSA VERDE
1 small onion, quartered
1 bunch coriander
5 ml/1 tsp crushed garlic
90 ml/6 tbsp olive oil

root ginger

onion

king prawns

white wine

garlic

olive oil

lime

coriander

1 Combine the white wine, ginger and garlic in a medium bowl. Add the prawns, turning to coat them in the marinade. Cover and chill for 4–6

2 Make the salsa. Chop the onion roughly in a food processor. Add the coriander and garlic and process until finely chopped. With the motor running, pour in the oil through the feeder tube of the processor. When the salsa is thick and creamy, scrape it into a serving bowl. Preheat the grill. Line the grill pan with foil.

3 Place half the prawns on the grill pan and cook for 5–6 minutes, turning them over halfway through cooking. Repeat with the remaining prawns. Divide the prawns among four plates. Cut the limes in half lengthways, then into wedges. Press the long edge of each wedge into the chopped coriander. Place two wedges on each plate. Serve with the salsa verde.

Smoked Salmon Terrine with Lemons

Lemons can be cut and sliced in so many ways. This smoked salmon terrine gives a time-honoured accompaniment an intriguing new twist.

Serves 6

INGREDIENTS
4 sheets of leaf gelatine
60 ml/4 tbsp water
400 g/14 oz smoked salmon, sliced
300 g/11 oz/1½ cups cream cheese
120 ml/4 fl oz/½ cup crème fraîche
30 ml/2 tbsp dill mustard
juice of 1 lime

FOR THE GARNISH
2 lemons
piece of muslin
raffia, for tying

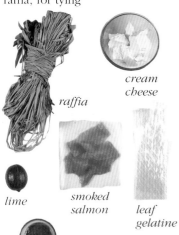

raffia

cream cheese

lime

smoked salmon

leaf gelatine

dill mustard

lemons

crème fraîche

1 Soak the gelatine in the water in a small bowl until softened. Meanwhile, line a 450 g/1 lb loaf tin with clear film. Use some of the smoked salmon to line the tin, laying the slices widthways across the bottom and up the sides, and leaving enough overlap to fold over the top of the filling.

2 Set aside enough of the remaining smoked salmon to make a middle layer the length of the tin. Chop the rest finely by hand or in a food processor. Beat together the cream cheese, crème fraîche and dill mustard with the chopped smoked salmon until everything is well combined.

3 Squeeze out the gelatine and melt gently in a small saucepan with the lime juice. Add to the smoked salmon mixture and mix thoroughly. Spoon half the mixture into the lined tin. Lay the reserved smoked salmon slices across the mixture, then spoon on the rest of the filling and smooth the top.

4 Tap the tin on the work surface to expel any trapped air. Fold over the overhanging salmon slices to cover the top. Cover with clear film and chill for at least 4 hours.

5 Make the garnish. Cut 1 lemon in half widthways. Wrap each half in a square of muslin. Gather the muslin at the rounded end of the lemon and tie neatly with raffia.

6 Cut a small "V" from the side of the other lemon. Repeat at 5 mm/¼ in intervals. Turn out the terrine, then slice. Garnish with muslin-wrapped lemons and lemon "leaves".

Crab Charlottes with Spring Onion Brushes

Spring onion brushes are traditionally served with Chinese food but make an equally effective garnish for these crab charlottes.

Serves 4

INGREDIENTS
11 spring onions
200 g/7 oz/scant 1 cup butter, melted
8 slices of white bread, crusts removed
300 g/11 oz drained, canned or fresh boiled crab meat
salt and freshly ground black pepper

butter

crab meat

spring onions

white bread

COOK'S TIP
Prepared in this way, spring onions are perfect for brushing a marinade over barbecued food. They can also be served with crispy duck and Chinese pancakes, and used to dip in the hoisin sauce.

1 Start by making the garnish. Trim 8 of the spring onions, removing the roots and bulbs. Cut off the tops at an angle to give a total length of about 15 cm/6 in.

4 Using a biscuit cutter, stamp out rounds from the bread to fit the bottom and top of the moulds. Cut the remaining bread into 2 cm/¾ in strips, and trim to the height of the moulds.

2 Using a fine-bladed knife make 5 cm/2 in lengthways cuts in the white part of a spring onion. Keep the cuts parallel and as close together as you can. Prepare the remaining trimmed spring onions in the same way. Place them in a bowl of chilled water and chill for at least 4 hours until curled.

5 Dip the bread rounds for the bases in melted butter and drop into the moulds. Dip the bread fingers in butter and use to line the sides.

3 Preheat the oven to 200°C/400°F/Gas 6. Chop the remaining spring onions and cook in 15 ml/1 tbsp of the butter for 3–4 minutes. Allow to cool. Use a little of the remaining butter to grease four large dariole moulds.

6 Mix the crab meat with the cooked spring onions. Season, then use to fill each mould. Dip the remaining bread rounds in butter and put on top of the filling. Bake on a baking sheet for about 20 minutes. Turn out and garnish each one with two brushes.

Tomato Soup with Swirled Cream

A swirl of cream is the classic finish for tomato soup. The technique is simplicity itself and works equally well on a savoury or sweet sauce.

Serves 8

INGREDIENTS
15 ml/1 tbsp olive oil
2 onions, chopped
225 g/8 oz floury potatoes, peeled and chopped
1.5 kg/3–3½ lb flavoursome tomatoes, peeled, seeded and chopped
900 ml/1½ pints/3¾ cups vegetable stock
1 bunch basil, roughly chopped
175 ml/6 fl oz/¾ cup crème fraîche
salt and freshly ground black pepper
150 ml/¼ pint/⅔ cup single cream, to garnish

basil

onion

crème fraîche

tomatoes

potato

single cream

olive oil

1 Heat the olive oil in a large saucepan, add the onions, cover and cook over a low heat for 10 minutes. Add the potato, replace the lid and cook for 5 minutes more. Stir in the tomatoes and vegetable stock.

2 Bring to the boil, then simmer for 35–40 minutes. Add the basil and seasoning. Purée in a food processor, then return to a clean pan and whisk in the crème fraîche. Heat without boiling, then ladle into warm soup bowls.

3 Pour the cream into a jug with a good pouring lip. Pour a swirl on to the surface of each bowl of soup.

4 Draw the tip of a fine skewer quickly backwards and forwards through the cream, to create a pattern.

Chicken Liver Pâté with Tomato Finger Fans

Tomato fans make an unusual garnish for this delicious pâté.

Serves 6

INGREDIENTS
30 ml/2 tbsp olive oil
1 onion, chopped
15 ml/1 tbsp chopped fresh
  thyme
225 g/8 oz chicken livers,
  trimmed
120 ml/4 fl oz/½ cup ruby port
120 ml/4 fl oz/½ cup double
  cream
salt and freshly ground black
  pepper

FOR THE GARNISH
5 firm tomatoes
flat leaf parsley sprigs

chicken livers   *double cream*

ruby port   *olive oil*

tomatoes   *onion*

parsley   *thyme*

1 Heat the oil in a frying pan. Add the onion and thyme and sauté for 5 minutes, then cover and cook for 10 minutes. Add the chicken livers and sauté for 4–5 minutes until brown but still slightly soft. Remove the chicken livers. Stir the ruby port into the pan and cook until reduced by half.

2 Purée the chicken livers and wine mixture in a food processor until smooth. Cool. Whip the cream to soft peaks and fold into the purée. Season to taste. Spoon the pâté into a serving dish; smooth the top. Chill for 3 hours.

3 Make the garnish. Cut the tomatoes into quarters. Hold each quarter skin-side down and use the knife to scoop out the pulp and seeds.

4 Make four cuts down the length of each tomato quarter, leaving about 1 cm/½ in intact at the top. Turn the tomato over and fan out the fingers. Top each tomato fan with a sprig of parsley. Serve a portion of pâté garnished with tomato fans.

Tarragon Chicken with Caramelized Onions

Served with slivers of herb butter, this makes a meal fit for any special celebration.

Serves 4

INGREDIENTS
4 skinless, boneless chicken
  breasts, about 175 g/6 oz each
2 onions, thinly sliced
2 garlic cloves, crushed
60 ml/4 tbsp chopped fresh
  tarragon
juice of 2 oranges
45 ml/3 tbsp sunflower oil
15 ml/1 tbsp soft brown sugar
60 ml/4 tbsp white wine
75 g/3 oz/⅓ cup butter
salt and freshly ground black
  pepper

FOR THE HERB BUTTER
115 g/4 oz/½ cup butter,
  softened
60 ml/4 tbsp orange juice
60 ml/4 tbsp chopped fresh
  tarragon

butter

white wine

oranges

onions

garlic

soft light brown sugar

tarragon

sunflower oil

chicken breasts

1 First, make the herb butter. Put the butter in a bowl. Gradually beat in the orange juice, then add the tarragon. Cut a 25 × 20 cm/10 × 8 in piece of greaseproof paper. Spoon the herb butter on to the paper in a broad line.

2 Fold the edge of the paper over the butter and pat down lightly. Roll the paper over the butter, squeezing it gently to form a long even roll.

3 Twist the ends of the paper to form a cracker, then chill the herb butter until firm.

4 Place the chicken, onions, garlic and half the tarragon in a bowl, with the orange juice. Marinate for 4 hours. Remove the chicken from the marinade. Heat 15 ml/1 tbsp oil in a frying pan. Add the onions and marinade. Cover and simmer for 15 minutes.

5 Add the sugar to the pan and cook, uncovered, for 15 minutes. Meanwhile, heat the remaining oil in another frying pan and brown the chicken. Lower the heat and cook for 10–12 minutes, turning halfway through. Place the chicken on a plate and keep hot.

6 Pour the wine into the pan. Stir well and cook until it has reduced by two-thirds. Whisk in small pieces of the butter. Add the remaining tarragon. Cook for 2–3 minutes, season and pour over the chicken breasts. Serve topped with slices of herb butter and accompanied with caramelized onions.

Port and Orange Duck with Cucumber Ribbons

Cucumber is wonderfully versatile. Here it provides an impressive garnish, worthy of this delicious orange-flavoured roast duck.

Serves 4–6

INGREDIENTS
1 duck, about 2.5–2.75 kg/
   5½–6 lb
60 ml/4 tbsp red wine
30 ml/2 tbsp plain flour
shredded rind and juice of
   4 large oranges
175 ml/6 fl oz/¾ cup ruby port
salt and freshly ground black
   pepper
1 cucumber, to garnish

orange

plain flour

red wine

duck

cucumber

ruby port

COOK'S TIP
Cucumber ribbons, marinated in a little rice wine vinegar and mixed with chopped parsley, make an interesting addition to a salad.

1 Preheat the oven to 230°C/450°F/ Gas 8. Weigh the duck and calculate the cooking time at 30 minutes per 450 g/1 lb. Pat the duck dry. Prick the skin all over with a fork, rub in a generous amount of salt and pepper, then place the duck on a rack in a roasting tin. Roast for 15 minutes, then lower the oven temperature to 190°C/375°F/ Gas 5 and cook for the remainder of the calculated time, basting occasionally.

4 Gradually whisk in the orange juice. Simmer gently for 10 minutes.

2 Place the duck on a heated platter and leave to rest in a warm place for 20 minutes. Drain the fat from the roasting tin, leaving behind the sediment and meat juices.

5 Meanwhile make the garnish. Cut the cucumber into 5 cm/2 in lengths, then cut lengthways into quarters. Make 6–7 fine horizontal cuts into the cucumber pieces, leaving 1 cm/½ in intact at one end.

3 Transfer the roasting tin to the hob. Add the red wine, stirring to incorporate the sediment. Cook until the wine has almost evaporated. Sprinkle in the flour and cook, stirring, for 2 minutes.

6 Fold each slice over to form a loop, starting at the top and working down, until 5–6 loops are made. Place skin-side up on the platter with the duck. Add the port to the orange sauce and season to taste. Strain into a warm jug and stir in the orange rind. Serve at once, with the duck.

Fillet Steak with Green Peppercorns and a Fluted Mushroom Garnish

Fluted mushrooms are a traditional garnish for steak – they are surprisingly easy to make.

Serves 4

INGREDIENTS
30 ml/2 tbsp green peppercorns
4 x 175 g/6 oz fillet steaks
25 g/1 oz/2 tbsp butter
15 ml/1 tbsp sunflower oil
45 ml/3 tbsp brandy
175 ml/6 fl oz/¾ cup beef stock
150 ml/¼ pint/⅔ cup double
  cream
salt and freshly ground black
  pepper

FOR THE GARNISH
4 large button mushrooms
25 g/1 oz/2 tbsp butter

double cream

green peppercorns

brandy

button mushrooms

fillet steak

butter

sunflower oil

1 Prepare the mushrooms for the garnish. Holding a mushroom by the stem, use a fine knife to cut a curved groove from the centre of the cap to the edge.

2 Turning the mushroom slightly each time, make several similar grooves, each following the line of the first. Trim the stem of the mushroom level with the base of the cap. Repeat with the remaining mushrooms. Set aside.

3 Lightly crush the peppercorns. Press half the peppercorns on to both sides of all the steaks. Heat the butter with the oil in a frying pan and cook two steaks for 5–7 minutes, turning over halfway through. Cook the other two steaks and keep hot.

4 Pour off any fat from the pan. Add the brandy, stirring to incorporate the sediment. Cook until most of the liquid has evaporated. Pour in the stock, bring to the boil and cook until reduced by half. Strain into a small saucepan, add the cream and remaining peppercorns and heat through without boiling. Season to taste. Heat the butter for the garnish in a small frying pan until hot and sauté the fluted mushrooms until golden and tender. Spoon the sauce over the steak, top with the fluted mushrooms and serve at once.

Tuna Steaks with a Tomato Salsa and Red Pepper Bundles

Red pepper bundles, tied together with bright green chives, make a colourful savoury garnish.

Serves 4

INGREDIENTS
45 ml/3 tbsp olive oil
15 ml/1 tbsp lemon juice
dash of Tabasco sauce
4 x 175 g/6 oz tuna steaks
225 g/8 oz tomatoes, quartered
  and deseeded
115 g/4 oz/½ cup sun-dried
  tomatoes in oil, drained, plus
  5 ml/1 tsp oil from the jar
30 ml/2 tbsp snipped fresh basil
  leaves
salt and freshly ground black
  pepper

FOR THE GARNISH
1 red pepper
8 long chives, wilted

sun-dried
tomatoes   Tabasco
                      sauce

chives   basil

        tuna steaks

red pepper
        olive
        oil
lemon   tomatoes

1 Mix 30 ml/2 tbsp olive oil, the lemon juice and Tabasco sauce in a bowl. Add the tuna, turn to coat well in the marinade, then cover and set aside to marinate for about 30 minutes.

2 Meanwhile make the salsa. Cut the fresh and sun-dried tomatoes into 5 mm/¼ in dice, put in a small bowl and mix well. Add the sun-dried tomato oil, basil and seasoning and toss together well.

3 Heat the remaining olive oil in a large frying pan and cook the tuna steaks, in batches if necessary, for about 8–10 minutes, turning halfway through.

4 Cut the pepper into sticks. Tie together with chives in bundles of 8–10. Pour the salsa over the tuna and garnish with the bundles.

Chicken Satay with Lime Garnishes

Limes provide a delightful colour contrast.

Serves 4–6

INGREDIENTS
4 skinless, boneless chicken
  breasts
2 limes and 4–6 coriander
  sprigs, to garnish

FOR THE MARINADE
1 small onion, finely chopped
15 ml/1 tbsp finely grated or
  crushed fresh root ginger
15 ml/1 tbsp crushed garlic
30 ml/2 tbsp dark soy sauce
10 ml/2 tsp ground coriander
5 ml/1 tsp ground cumin
15 ml/1 tbsp soft dark brown
  sugar
15 ml/1 tbsp sunflower oil

FOR THE PEANUT DIP
115 g/4 oz/½ cup smooth
  peanut butter
100 ml/3½ fl oz/⅓ cup coconut
  milk
30 ml/2 tbsp fish sauce
15 ml/1 tbsp fresh lime juice
dash of Tabasco sauce

peanut butter
coconut milk
root ginger
chicken breast
onion
soft dark brown sugar
fish sauce
ground coriander
coriander
limes
ground cumin
garlic
soy sauce

1 Cut the chicken breasts into 2 cm x 5 mm/¾ x ¼ in strips. Mix all the marinade ingredients in a bowl, add the chicken strips and toss until coated. Cover and marinate in the fridge for 4 hours or preferably overnight.

2 Make the dip by mixing all the ingredients in a bowl. Cover and set aside for at least 1 hour to allow the flavours to combine.

3 Using a cannelle knife, cut stripes lengthways down the skin of one of the limes at 1 cm/½ in intervals. Cut the lime into 5 mm/¼ in slices. Make a cut from the centre to the edge of each slice; twist to an "S" shape.

4 Cut the remaining lime in half lengthways and place cut-side down. Make three V-shaped cuts into the lime halves, one below the other and push each wedge out slightly to give a stepped effect. Preheat the grill or prepare the barbecue if using. Drain the chicken strips, reserving the marinade. Thread on to wooden skewers.

5 Either cook in a hot frying pan, place under a grill, or barbecue over moderately hot coals until tender, turning frequently and brushing occasionally with the reserved marinade. Serve garnished with the limes and coriander sprigs. Accompany with the peanut dip.

Rack of Lamb with Redcurrant Bunches

Bunches of redcurrants tied with chives provide a strong colour contrast to glazed rack of lamb.

Serves 4

INGREDIENTS
45 ml/3 tbsp redcurrant jelly
5 ml/1 tsp wholegrain mustard
2 best ends of lamb, each with
  6 chops, trimmed of all fat
45 ml/3 tbsp sunflower oil
120 ml/4 fl oz/½ cup red wine
120 ml/4 fl oz/½ cup stock
  or water
salt and freshly ground black
  pepper

FOR THE GARNISH
8 small bunches of redcurrants
4 chives, wilted

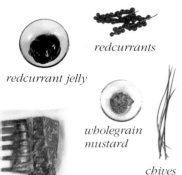

redcurrant jelly

redcurrants

wholegrain mustard

chives

best end of lamb

red wine

sunflower oil

stock

1 Preheat the oven to 200°C/400°F/ Gas 6. Melt the redcurrant jelly with the mustard in a small saucepan, stirring occasionally. Brush half the mixture over the lamb and set the rest aside. Heat the oil in a roasting tin, add the lamb and sear quickly on all sides until browned.

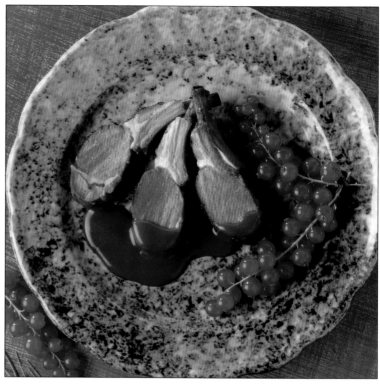

2 Brush the remaining redcurrant glaze over the lamb, then place in the oven for 20–30 minutes or until cooked to your taste. Transfer the lamb to a warm platter, loosely cover with foil and allow to rest for 10 minutes.

3 Drain the fat from the roasting tin, leaving the sediment behind. Place the tin over a medium heat, add the red wine and stir thoroughly. Cook until most of the liquid has evaporated, then add the stock or water. Bring to the boil, lower the heat and simmer for 5 minutes. Season, strain into a sauce-boat and keep hot.

4 Wrap the chives several times around the redcurrant stems, tie neatly in a knot and trim the ends. Make four bunches in this way. Carve the lamb into cutlets, arrange on four dinner plates and spoon over a little of the sauce. Garnish individual plates with the redcurrant bunches.

Pork and Apple Bake with Sautéed Potatoes

Crispy sautéed potato cubes frame portions of pork topped with apple and a crumb crust.

Serves 4

INGREDIENTS
butter, for greasing
1 medium onion, thickly sliced
15 ml/1 tbsp chopped
    fresh sage
500 g/1¼ lb boneless pork loin
    chops, trimmed of all fat
2 eating apples
150 ml/¼ pint/⅔ cup white
    wine
45 ml/3 tbsp fresh breadcrumbs
45 ml/3 tbsp freshly grated
    Parmesan cheese

FOR THE GARNISH
1 large waxy potato, peeled
30 ml/2 tbsp sunflower oil
fresh sage leaves

Parmesan cheese

onion

white wine   *breadcrumbs*

pork loin chops   *eating apples*

potato

1 Preheat the oven to 200°C/400°F/Gas 6. Butter a large ovenproof dish and spread out the onion slices and sage on the bottom. Arrange the pork chops in a single layer over the top.

2 Quarter, peel and core the apples. Slice them thickly and arrange on top of the pork. Pour over the white wine. Mix the breadcrumbs and Parmesan together and sprinkle evenly over the apple. Bake for 1–1½ hours until the pork is tender and the topping is crisp and golden.

3 Make the garnish. Square off the sides of the potato. Cut into 1 cm/½ in slices, then stack two or three slices together and cut into 1 cm/½ in cubes. Place in a colander, rinse under cold water, drain and pat dry.

4 Heat the oil in a large frying pan. Add the potato, turning it in the oil to coat. Cook, tossing occasionally, for 10–15 minutes until the cubes are golden brown and tender. Drain briefly on kitchen paper. Spoon a portion of the bake on to each plate and arrange the potato cubes in lines spreading outwards. Serve, garnished with sage.

Spicy Trout with a Herb Bouquet

Tender trout, cooked in a chilli and rock salt crust, does not need an elaborate garnish. A simple bouquet of fresh herbs is ideal.

Serves 2

INGREDIENTS
2 x 375 g/12 oz whole rainbow
    trout
1 lemon, sliced

FOR THE CRUST
60 ml/4 tbsp rock salt
10 ml/2 tsp chilli powder
15 ml/1 tbsp paprika
5 ml/1 tsp cayenne pepper
2.5 ml/½ tsp freshly ground
    black pepper
30 ml/2 tbsp olive oil

FOR THE GARNISH
1 bunch mixed herbs, such as
    parsley, chives, dill and
    rosemary
raffia, for tying

rainbow trout

olive oil

rock salt

parsley

dill

rosemary

lemon

raffia

chilli powder

paprika

cayenne pepper

1 Combine all the dry ingredients for the crust in a small bowl. Add the oil and mix to a thick paste.

2 Remove the fins from the trout. Rinse and pat dry. Pierce the fish with a knife, on both sides, at 2.5 cm/1 in intervals. Divide a quarter of the paste between the fish cavities, then put the lemon slices inside. Coat both trout with the remaining paste. Preheat the grill. Put the trout in a foil-lined grill pan. Grill for 15–20 minutes or until tender; turn halfway through cooking.

3 Meanwhile make the garnish. Starting with several long-stemmed pieces of parsley, make up a bouquet, adding chives, dill and rosemary (or other herbs of your own choice). If some of the herbs are in flower, so much the better. Tie a long piece of raffia around the bouquet, about three-quarters of the way down. Wind the raffia around several times to give a wide band and finish with a knot or large bow. Cut the herb stems level and trim the raffia ends at an angle.

4 Check that the trout is cooked by inserting a knife into the thickest part; the flesh should just flake. Carefully transfer the trout to a warm platter. Garnish with the herb bouquet and serve at once.

Beef Stir-fry with a Cucumber Flower

A cucumber flower is a stunning Chinese garnish; the perfect decoration for a tasty stir-fry.

Serves 2–3

INGREDIENTS
15 ml/1 tbsp sunflower oil
5 ml/1 tsp crushed garlic
30 ml/2 tbsp grated root ginger
45 ml/3 tbsp clear honey
30 ml/2 tbsp fresh lime juice
45 ml/3 tbsp soy sauce
1 red onion, thinly sliced
1 red pepper, thinly sliced
115 g/4 oz broccoli florets
115 g/4 oz baby corn, halved
175 g/6 oz rump steak, trimmed
  and cut into 4 cm/1½ in strips
115 g/4 oz oyster mushrooms,
  sliced
75 g/3 oz beansprouts
salt and freshly ground black
  pepper
15 cm/6 in piece cucumber,
  to garnish

broccoli
rump steak
red pepper
baby corn
beansprouts
lime
oyster mushrooms
red onion
cucumber
root ginger

1 First, make the garnish. Cut the cucumber in half lengthways and remove the seeds. Place each half cut-side down and cut at an angle into 7.5 cm/3 in lengths. Cut into fine slices, stopping 5 mm/¼ in short of the cut side, so that the slices remain attached.

2 Fan the slices out. Turn in alternate slices to form a loop. Bend the length into a semi-circle with the loops on the outside so that they resemble petals. Make more flowers in the same way.

3 Heat the sunflower oil in a wok. Mix the garlic, ginger, honey, lime juice and soy sauce in a bowl, add them to the wok and cook for 30 seconds. Add the onion and red pepper and stir-fry for 2 minutes.

4 Add the broccoli, baby corn and beef and stir-fry for 3–4 minutes. Finally add the oyster mushrooms and beansprouts. Stir-fry for a further 2 minutes. Adjust seasoning and add more soy sauce if necessary. Serve garnished with the cucumber flowers.

Spicy Tomato Tart with Tomato Roses

Serve this chilli-flavoured tomato tart hot or cold. Echo the theme with tomato roses.

Serves 8–10

INGREDIENTS
300 g/11 oz/2¾ cups self-raising flour
200 g/7 oz/scant 1 cup butter, diced
45–60 ml/3–4 tbsp cold water
salt and freshly ground black pepper

FOR THE FILLING
30 ml/2 tbsp olive oil
2 onions, thinly sliced
1 garlic clove, crushed
1.5 kg/3–3½ lb tomatoes, peeled and chopped
2 dried chillies, seeded and chopped
120 ml/4 fl oz/½ cup passata (sieved tomatoes)
30 ml/2 tbsp caster sugar

FOR THE GARNISH
3 firm tomatoes
sprig of basil

onion

self-raising flour

passata

basil

tomatoes

butter

garlic

dried chillies

1 Place the flour, salt and butter together in a food processor, process until the mixture resembles bread-crumbs. Add the water and process for another 5–10 seconds to mix together. Turn out on to a floured work surface and knead lightly to a firm dough. Wrap in clear film and chill. Preheat the oven to 190°C/375°F/Gas 5.

4 Pour the tomato sauce into the pastry case, spreading it out evenly. Return the tomato tart to the oven for 20–25 minutes.

2 Make the filling. Heat the olive oil in a large frying pan, add the onions and garlic and fry for 10 minutes. Stir in the chopped tomatoes and chillies. Bring to the boil, lower the heat and simmer for 20–25 minutes until thickened. Add the passata and sugar and simmer for 5 minutes more. Add salt and pepper to taste and allow to cool.

3 On a lightly floured surface, roll out the pastry and line a deep 25 cm/10 in flan tin. Prick the base of the pastry, line with non-stick baking paper and fill with baking beans. Bake blind for 15 minutes, then remove the beans and paper. Return the flan case to the oven for 5 minutes more.

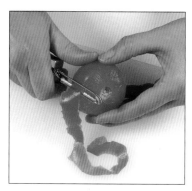

5 Meanwhile, make the garnish. Using a swivel-blade peeler and starting at the base of one of the tomatoes, peel it in one long continuous strip. Work care-fully and slowly to avoid breaking the strip, and keep the peel as thin as possi-ble. Reserve the peeled tomato for using in a soup or sauce.

6 With the skin side out, and starting at the stem end, coil the peel loosely to within 2 cm/¾ in of the end. Set the coil upright so that it resembles a rose bud and tuck the end loosely under-neath. Repeat with remaining tomatoes. Serve the tomato tart hot or at room temperature. Garnish with the tomato roses and the basil sprig.

Noodles with Lemon Grass, Chillies and Herbs

Traditional Thai ingredients provide a colourful contrast to a tasty noodle stew.

Serves 6

INGREDIENTS
30 ml/2 tbsp sunflower oil
1 onion, thickly sliced
1 lemon grass stem, finely chopped
15 ml/1 tbsp Thai red curry paste
3 courgettes, thickly sliced
115 g/4 oz Savoy cabbage, thickly sliced
2 carrots, thickly sliced
150 g/5 oz broccoli, stem sliced thickly and head separated into florets
2 x 400 ml/14 fl oz cans coconut milk
475 ml/16 fl oz/2 cups vegetable stock
150 g/5 oz egg noodles
15 ml/1 tbsp fish sauce
30 ml/2 tbsp soy sauce
60 ml/4 tbsp chopped fresh coriander

FOR THE GARNISH
2 lemon grass stems
1 bunch coriander
8–10 small red chillies

soy sauce
coconut milk
Savoy cabbage
Thai red curry paste
onion
lemon grass
coriander
courgettes
fish sauce
red chillies
broccoli
carrots
egg noodles

1 Heat the oil in a large saucepan or wok. Add the onion, lemon grass and Thai red curry paste. Stirring occasionally, cook for 5–10 minutes until the onion has softened.

2 Add the courgettes, cabbage, carrots and broccoli stems. Using two spoons, toss the vegetables with the onion mixture and cook gently for a further 5 minutes.

3 Stir in the coconut milk and vegetable stock and bring to the boil. Add the noodles and the broccoli florets, lower the heat and simmer gently for 20 minutes.

4 Meanwhile, make the garnish. Split the lemon grass lengthways through the root. Gather the coriander into a small bouquet and lay it on a platter, following the curve of the rim.

5 Tuck the lemon grass halves into the bouquet and add the chillies to resemble flowers. Stir the fish sauce, soy sauce and chopped coriander into the noodle mixture. Spoon on to the platter, taking care not to disturb the herb bouquet.

Creamy Risotto with Asparagus

Fine asparagus spears look great gathered in a bundle and tied with a spring onion stem.

Serves 4

INGREDIENTS
1.5 litres/2½ pints/6 cups
  vegetable stock
30 ml/2 tbsp olive oil
1 onion, finely chopped
2 garlic cloves, crushed
225 g/8 oz/1 generous cup
  arborio rice
150 ml/¼ pint/⅔ cup white wine
225 g/8 oz asparagus spears,
  cut into 2.5 cm/1 in pieces
50 g/2 oz/¼ cup butter
45 ml/3 tbsp freshly grated
  Parmesan cheese
salt and freshly ground black
  pepper

FOR THE GARNISH
12 slender asparagus spears
4 long green spring onion
  stems, wilted

arborio rice
asparagus spears
onion
butter
garlic
Parmesan cheese
spring onions
olive oil
white wine

1 Heat the stock to simmering point in a saucepan. In a separate, large pan, heat the olive oil and fry the onion and garlic for 10 minutes until softened but not coloured. Add the rice, stir to coat the grains in oil and cook for 2–3 minutes. Pour in the white wine and cook until absorbed.

2 Ladle in about a quarter of the hot stock. Lower the heat to a gentle simmer and cook, stirring frequently, until it has all been absorbed. Repeat with another ladleful of stock, adding the chopped asparagus at the same time and continuing to stir. Add the remaining stock in the same way, each time allowing all the stock to be absorbed before adding more. This should take 20–25 minutes.

3 Meanwhile, make the garnish. Cook the asparagus in boiling lightly salted water until tender, then drain. Place 3 asparagus spears together, positioning them 2 cm/¾ in below one another. Tie the spears together with a wilted spring onion stem. Make three more asparagus bundles in the same way.

4 Trim the base of each bundle of spears across at an angle. Trim the ends of the spring onion ties neatly. Stir the butter and Parmesan into the risotto and serve at once, garnishing each portion with an asparagus bundle.

Warm Broad Bean Salad with Filo Stars

Skinning broad beans is time-consuming but worth it for the beautiful colour. Serve this delectable warm salad with spicy filo stars.

Serves 6

INGREDIENTS
900 g/2 lb shelled broad beans
30 ml/2 tbsp olive oil
1 red onion, finely diced
2 garlic cloves, crushed
1 courgette, finely diced
115 g/4 oz frozen or drained
  canned sweetcorn
4 tomatoes, peeled, seeded and
  finely chopped
salt and freshly ground black
  pepper

FOR THE GARNISH
3 filo pastry sheets
15 ml/1 tbsp sunflower oil
5 ml/1 tsp mild chilli powder

sweetcorn

chilli powder

olive oil

broad beans

courgette

filo pastry

garlic

red onion

sunflower oil

tomato

1 Preheat the oven to 200°C/400°F/ Gas 6. Bring a saucepan of water to the boil and blanch the broad beans for 2–3 minutes. Drain, refresh under cold running water and drain again. Pop the beans out of their skins and set them aside.

2 Heat the oil in a saucepan. Fry the onion and garlic gently until soft but not brown. Add the courgette and sweetcorn and cook for 10 minutes. Add the tomatoes and broad beans and cook for 2 minutes. Season and

3 Make the garnish. Lay out a sheet of filo pastry. Brush lightly with the oil. Sprinkle a third of the chilli powder over. Place another sheet of filo pastry on top and repeat. Repeat with the remaining sheet of filo pastry.

4 Using a large star cutter, stamp out six stars from the layered filo. Transfer them to a lightly oiled baking sheet and bake for 7–8 minutes, until golden and crisp. Serve the warm salad topped with the spicy filo stars.

Fennel Ravioli with Tartan Jackets

This ravioli has its own built-in garnish! Coloured stripes rolled into the pasta make this unusual dish a real show-stopper!

Serves 4–6

INGREDIENTS

FOR THE PLAIN PASTA
225 g/8 oz/2 cups strong white flour
2 size 1 eggs
1 size 1 egg yolk
15 ml/1 tbsp olive oil

FOR THE TOMATO PASTA
175 g/6 oz/1½ cups strong white flour
1 size 1 egg
1 size 1 egg yolk
30 ml/2 tbsp tomato purée

FOR THE SPINACH PASTA
175 g/6 oz/1½ cups strong white flour
1 size 1 egg
1 size 1 egg yolk
15 ml/1 tbsp spinach purée

FOR THE FILLING AND GARNISH
115 g/4 oz/½ cup butter
1 large fennel bulb
2 garlic cloves, crushed
120 ml/4 fl oz/½ cup double cream
200 g/7 oz Gorgonzola cheese, crumbled
salt and freshly ground black pepper

COOK'S TIP

Not all the ravioli need to have tartan jackets – leaving most of them plain and making just two tartan ravioli per person can be just as effective.

1 Place the flour, eggs, egg yolk and olive oil for the plain pasta, in a food processor and process until the dough forms a ball around the blade. If dry, add a little water. Knead briefly until smooth, place in a bowl, cover and allow to rest for an hour. Repeat with the tomato pasta ingredients and then with the spinach pasta ingredients.

fennel

Gorgonzola cheese

olive oil

strong white flour

spinach

eggs

double cream

2 Make the filling. Heat the butter in a frying pan. Set aside the fennel fronds to scatter over each serving, then dice the fennel bulb. Add to the pan with the garlic, cover and allow it to sweat gently for 10 minutes until tender. Stir in the cream and cheese. Cook for about 5 minutes, season to taste and then set aside to cool.

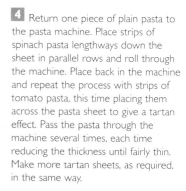

3 Divide the plain dough into small pieces and pass through a pasta machine, reducing the roller settings until the sheets are medium-thin. Place the finished sheets on a baking sheet dusted with flour and cover with a damp cloth and clear film to prevent it from drying out while you prepare the other pasta in the same way. On the final rolling, cut both the tomato and the spinach dough into fettucine (strips about 1 cm/½ in wide).

4 Return one piece of plain pasta to the pasta machine. Place strips of spinach pasta lengthways down the sheet in parallel rows and roll through the machine. Place back in the machine and repeat the process with strips of tomato pasta, this time placing them across the pasta sheet to give a tartan effect. Pass the pasta through the machine several times, each time reducing the thickness until fairly thin. Make more tartan sheets, as required, in the same way.

5 Place a finished sheet of pasta, on a lightly floured work surface. Cut into 6 cm/2 ½ in squares. Brush lightly with a little water. Place a teaspoon of the fennel mixture in the centre of each square.

6 Cut a second sheet of pasta into squares of the same size and place on top of the filled squares. Crimp the edges of each square with a fork or alternatively use a crimping wheel. Bring a large saucepan of lightly salted water to the boil. Cook the ravioli in batches for 5 minutes or until they rise to the surface of the water. Drain and serve at once, garnished with the reserved fennel fronds.

Roast Peppers and Courgettes

Colourful tomato suns complement a grilled mixed pepper salad.

Serves 4

INGREDIENTS
2 red peppers, quartered and
   seeded
2 yellow peppers, quartered and
   seeded
2 courgettes
45 ml/3 tbsp olive oil
15 ml/1 tbsp white wine vinegar
30 ml/2 tbsp chopped fresh
   coriander
salt and freshly ground black
   pepper

FOR THE GARNISH
8 red cherry tomatoes

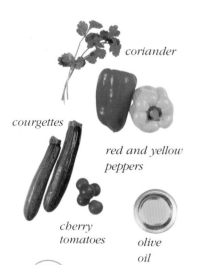

coriander

courgettes

red and yellow peppers

cherry tomatoes

olive oil

white wine vinegar

1 Preheat the grill to medium. Put the peppers flesh-side down on a foil-lined grill pan and grill for 10–15 minutes until blackened and soft. Place in a plastic bag, close tightly and leave to cool. Peel off the skin from the peppers and cut the flesh into 1 cm/½ in strips.

2 Using a swivel-blade peeler, cut the courgettes into ribbons. Heat 15 ml/ 1 tbsp of the olive oil in a frying pan, and sauté the courgettes for 2–3 minutes. Place in a bowl with the peppers. Whisk together the remaining oil, vinegar and coriander. Pour over the vegetables, season and toss lightly.

3 Make the garnish. Place a tomato stem-side down. Cut lightly into the skin across the top, edging the knife down towards base on either side. Turn the tomato through 90° and repeat, turning and cutting until the skin has been cut into eight separate segments, joined at the base.

4 Carefully slide the top of the knife under the point of each segment and ease the skin away towards the base, stopping just short. Gently fold the petals back to mimic the sun's rays. Make more suns in the same way. Spoon the salad on to individual plates, adding two tomato suns to each.

Creamy Pasta with Parmesan Curls

Several perfectly formed curls of Parmesan give a plate of creamy pasta a lift.

Serves 4–6

INGREDIENTS
250 g/9 oz dried campanelle pasta
30 ml/2 tbsp olive oil
250 g/9 oz/1¼ cups mascarpone cheese
200 ml/7 fl oz/scant 1 cup crème fraîche
75 g/3 oz/¾ cup freshly grated Parmesan cheese
115 g/4 oz sun-dried tomatoes in oil, drained and thinly sliced
salt and freshly ground black pepper

FOR THE GARNISH
1 piece of Parmesan cheese, about 175 g/6 oz

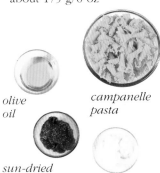

olive oil

sun-dried tomatoes

Parmesan cheese

campanelle pasta

mascarpone cheese

crème fraîche

1 Unless you are an old hand at making Parmesan curls, do this first, before cooking the pasta. Holding a swivel-blade peeler at a 45° angle, draw it steadily across the block of Parmesan cheese to form a curl. Make several curls, depending on the number of guests being served.

2 Bring a large saucepan of lightly salted water to the boil. Add the olive oil and pasta, stir and cook according to the instructions on the packet.

3 Meanwhile, melt the mascarpone and crème fraîche together in a second saucepan. Add the Parmesan and sun-dried tomatoes and cook over a low heat for 5 minutes. Season with plenty of black pepper and a little salt.

4 Drain the pasta, return it to the pan and pour the sauce over. Toss to mix together thoroughly. Serve on individual plates, adding a few Parmesan curls to each portion.

Aubergine Bake with Leek Haystacks

Stacks of golden leek look marvellous with this Mediterranean bake.

Serves 4–6

INGREDIENTS
2 x 400 g/14 oz cans chopped
 tomatoes
5 ml/1 tsp white wine vinegar
15 ml/1 tbsp caster sugar
30 ml/2 tbsp pesto
3 medium aubergines
90 ml/6 tbsp olive oil
butter, for greasing
350 g/12 oz mozzarella cheese,
 thinly sliced
45 g/3 tbsp fresh breadcrumbs
30 g/1 oz/¼ cup freshly grated
 Parmesan cheese
salt and freshly ground black
 pepper

FOR THE GARNISH
1 large leek
30 ml/2 tbsp plain flour
oil, for deep-frying

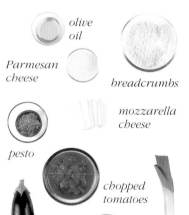

olive oil

Parmesan cheese

breadcrumbs

mozzarella cheese

pesto

chopped tomatoes

aubergine

white wine vinegar

leek

1 Pour the canned tomatoes into a saucepan. Bring to the boil, then simmer for 20 minutes. Purée in a food processor. Return to the pan and add the vinegar, sugar, pesto and seasoning. Cook for 5 minutes, then remove the pan from the heat.

2 Cut the aubergines lengthways into 5 mm/¼ in thick slices. Heat 30 ml/ 2 tbsp of the olive oil in a large frying pan. Fry the aubergine slices, in batches, for 5–6 minutes until golden, turning halfway through and adding more oil as required. Drain on kitchen paper.

3 Preheat the oven to 200°C/400°F/ Gas 6. Butter a large shallow baking dish. Lay a third of the aubergine slices on the bottom of the dish, then spoon over a third of the tomato sauce.

4 Top with a third of the mozzarella slices. Make two more layers, using the remaining ingredients. Sprinkle the breadcrumbs and Parmesan evenly over the top. Bake for 35–40 minutes until golden and bubbling.

5 Meanwhile make the garnish. Slice the leek lengthways in half and then into quarters. Cut into 5 cm/2 in lengths and then into very fine julienne. Place in a bowl, sprinkle the flour over and toss to coat.

6 Just before the bake is ready, heat the oil to 160°C/325°F. Drop small spoonfuls of the floured leeks into the oil and cook for 30–45 seconds until golden. Drain on kitchen paper. Repeat with the remaining leeks. Serve the bake with a small stack of leeks on top of each portion.

Port Wine Jelly with Trailed Cream Hearts

There can be few more impressive desserts than this – dark, rich blackcurrant coulis swirled with cream hearts surrounds a sophisticated jelly.

Serves 6–8

INGREDIENTS
6 sheets of leaf gelatine
475 ml/16 fl oz/2 cups water
450 g/1 lb blackcurrants
225 g/8 oz/1 cup caster sugar
150 ml/¼ pint/⅔ cup ruby port
30 ml/2 tbsp crème de cassis
120 ml/4 fl oz/½ cup single
  cream, to decorate

single cream

ruby port

blackcurrants

leaf gelatine

caster sugar

crème de cassis

1 In a small bowl, soak the gelatine in 75 ml/5 tbsp of the water until soft. Place the blackcurrants, sugar and 300ml/ ½ pint/1¼ cups of the remaining water in a large saucepan. Bring to the boil, lower the heat and simmer for 20 minutes. Strain, reserving the cooking liquid in a large jug. Put half the blackcurrants in a bowl and pour over 60 ml/4 tbsp of the reserved cooking liquid. (Freeze the remaining blackcurrants for another day.) Set the bowl and jug aside.

COOK'S TIP
If you have trouble finding leaf gelatine it can be substituted with powdered gelatine. Use 5 ml/ 1 tsp for each gelatine leaf, and simply sprinkle over the port at the beginning of step 2.

2 Squeeze the water out of the gelatine and place in a small saucepan with the port, cassis and remaining water. Heat gently to dissolve the gelatine but do not allow the mixture to boil. Stir into the jug of blackcurrant liquid until well mixed.

4 Run a fine knife around each jelly. Dip each mould in hot water for 5–10 seconds, then turn the jelly out on to your hand. Place on a serving plate and spoon the coulis around the jelly.

3 Run 6–8 jelly moulds under cold water, drain and place in a roasting tin. Fill with the port mixture. Chill for at least 6 hours until set. Tip the bowl of blackcurrants into a food processor, purée until smooth, then pass through a fine sieve. Taste the coulis and adjust the sweetness.

5 Drop a little cream at intervals on to the coulis. Draw a cocktail stick through the cream dots, dragging each in turn into a heart shape. Serve the desserts immediately.

Raspberry Sorbet with a Soft Fruit Garland

This stunning fresh fruit and herb garnish creates a bold border for the scoops of sorbet.

Serves 6–8

INGREDIENTS
175 g/6 oz/¾ cup caster sugar
250 ml/8 fl oz/1 cup water
450 g/1 lb fresh or thawed
  frozen raspberries
strained juice of 1 orange

FOR THE DECORATION
1 bunch mint
selection of soft fruits,
  including strawberries,
  raspberries, redcurrants and
  blueberries

raspberries

orange   *caster sugar*

redcurrants   *blueberries*

mint   *strawberries*

COOK'S TIP
Make the sorbet in an ice cream maker, if you have one, following the manufacturer's instructions.

1 Heat the caster sugar with the water in a saucepan, until dissolved, stirring occasionally. Bring to the boil, then set aside to cool. Purée the raspberries with the orange juice in a blender or food processor, then use a wooden spoon to press through a sieve to remove any seeds.

2 Mix the syrup with the puréed raspberries and pour into a freezer container. Freeze for 2 hours or until ice crystals form around the edges. Whisk until smooth, then return to the freezer for 4 hours.

3 About 30 minutes before serving, transfer the sorbet to the fridge to soften slightly. Place a large sprig of mint on the rim of a serving plate, then build up a garland, using more sprigs.

4 Leaving on the leaves, cut the strawberries in half. Arrange on the mint with the other fruit. Place the fruits at different angles and link the leaves with strings of redcurrants. Place scoops of sorbet in the centre.

Lemon Mousse with Shortbread Hearts

Shortbread can be stamped out into any shape, baked and then lightly dusted with icing sugar. For a special occasion frosted rose petals can be used as a decoration in place of the lemon rind.

Serves 6–8

INGREDIENTS
4 sheets of leaf gelatine
60 ml/4 tbsp water
225 g/8 oz/1 cup mascarpone
  cheese
225 g/8 oz/1 cup fromage frais
45 ml/3 tbsp icing sugar, sifted
grated rind and juice of
  2 lemons
3 size 2 egg whites

FOR THE SHORTBREAD HEARTS
25 g/1 oz/¼ cup chopped
  almonds, toasted
75 g/3 oz/6 tbsp caster sugar
150 g/5 oz/1¼ cups plain flour
115 g/4 oz/½ cup butter, diced
sifted icing sugar, for dusting

chopped almonds
mascarpone cheese
leaf gelatine
eggs
lemon
fromage frais
plain flour
caster sugar
butter
icing sugar

1 Soak the gelatine in the water until soft. Beat the mascarpone, fromage frais and icing sugar together until fluffy. Squeeze out the water from the gelatine and melt with the lemon juice in a small saucepan. Cool slightly, then beat into the mascarpone mixture.

2 Whisk the egg whites until stiff. Fold into the mascarpone mixture, with half the lemon rind. Spoon into serving dishes and chill for 3–4 hours until set.

3 Meanwhile, make the shortbread hearts. Process the almonds and sugar in a processor until fine. Add the flour and mix. Add the butter and process until a dough forms. Turn out and knead lightly. Wrap in clear film and chill for 20 minutes. Preheat the oven to 180°C/350°F/Gas 4.

4 Line a baking sheet with baking parchment. Roll out the dough on a lightly floured surface to 5 mm/¼ in thick. Stamp out heart-shaped biscuits, put on the baking sheet and bake for 10–12 minutes. Cool. Dust with icing sugar. Top the mousse with remaining lemon rind and serve with the hearts.

Chocolate Mousse with Chocolate Curls

Dark, white and milk chocolate curls provide a finishing flourish for a sumptuous chocolate mousse with just a hint of ginger.

Serves 6–8

INGREDIENTS
450 g/1 lb plain chocolate,
  finely chopped
65 g/2½ oz/5 tbsp butter
200 g/7 oz/scant 1 cup caster
  sugar
6 eggs, separated
60 ml/4 tbsp ginger syrup (from
  a jar of preserved stem ginger)
100 ml/3½ fl oz/⅓ cup brandy

FOR THE DECORATION
115 g/4 oz plain chocolate or
  a mixture of plain, milk and
  white chocolate

plain chocolate

ginger syrup

brandy

caster sugar

eggs

butter

COOK'S TIP
The mousse can be made up to 3 days before it is to be served, provided it is kept in the fridge.

1 Melt the chocolate and butter with half the sugar in a bowl set over a saucepan of hot water. Remove the bowl from the pan and beat in the egg yolks, ginger syrup and brandy.

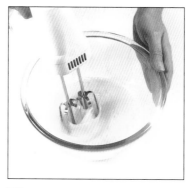

2 Whisk the egg whites in a large grease-free bowl until soft peaks form. Gradually add the remaining sugar, a spoonful at a time, whisking constantly until stiff and glossy.

3 Beat about a third of the egg whites into the chocolate mixture to lighten it, then fold in the remainder. Pour into 6–8 serving bowls or glasses and chill for 3–4 hours until set.

4 To make the decoration, melt the chocolate, beat it briefly, then pour on to a flat surface such as a baking sheet. Spread out with a palette knife until about 3 mm/⅛ in thick. Allow to cool until firm but pliable.

5 For a more dramatic effect make light and dark curls, using plain, milk and white chocolate. Pipe the melted chocolate in alternate rows, smooth each in turn with a palette knife and allow to firm before making the curls.

6 Hold a cheese slicer and place flat against the chocolate. Pull it gently towards you, scraping off a thin layer of chocolate so that it curls into a scroll. Work quickly or the chocolate will harden and splinter. Decorate the mousses just before serving.

Mango Ice Cream with Exotic Fruit Salad

Exotic fruits are now widely available: choose your fruits with care, taking colour, shape and taste into account, then use them to create your own still life next to a marvellous mango and ginger ice cream.

Serves 6–8

INGREDIENTS
2 large ripe mangoes, peeled and roughly chopped
2 pieces of preserved stem ginger plus 30 ml/2 tbsp ginger syrup
250 ml/8 fl oz/1 cup double cream

FOR THE DECORATION
1 star fruit, thickly sliced
1 mango, peeled and cut into wedges
1 cantaloupe melon, cut into wedges
6 strawberries, cut in half
1 small bunch frosted grapes

cantaloupe melon

mangoes

grapes

ginger syrup

star fruit

double cream

strawberries

stem ginger

1 Purée the mangoes in a food processor with the preserved ginger and ginger syrup, until smooth.

2 Whip the cream in a large bowl until it forms fairly firm peaks. Fold in the mango purée.

3 Transfer to a freezer container. Freeze for 2 hours, then beat with an electric mixer until smooth. Return the ice cream to the freezer and freeze for at least 8 hours. Or, freeze in an ice cream maker according to the manufacturer's instructions.

4 About 30 minutes before serving, transfer the ice cream to the fridge to soften slightly. Arrange the prepared fruit on individual plates and add two scoops of ice cream to each one.

Raspberries with a Tricolour Swirled Purée

Three fruit purées, swirled together, make a kaleidoscopic garnish for a nest of raspberries.

Serves 4–6

INGREDIENTS
200 g/7 oz raspberries
120 ml/4 fl oz/½ cup red wine
icing sugar, for dusting

FOR THE DECORATION
1 large mango, peeled and
  chopped
400 g/14 oz kiwi fruit, peeled
  and chopped
200 g/7 oz raspberries
icing sugar, to taste

red wine

icing sugar

mango

kiwi fruit

raspberries

COOK'S TIP
Purées can be prepared from any available fruit and freeze well, ready for making an easy last-minute garnish.

1 Place the raspberries in a bowl with the red wine and allow to macerate for about 2 hours.

2 Make the decoration. Purée the mango in a food processor, adding a little water if necessary. Press through a sieve into a bowl. Purée the kiwi fruit in the same way, then make a third purée from the remaining raspberries. Sweeten the purées with sifted icing sugar, if necessary.

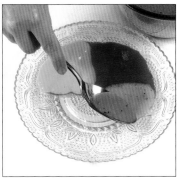

3 Spoon each purée on to a serving plate, separating the kiwi and mango with the raspberry purée as if creating a four-wedged pie. Gently tap the plate on the work surface to settle the purées against each other.

4 Using a skewer, draw a spiral outwards from the centre of the plate to the rim. Drain the macerated raspberries, pile them in the centre, and dust them heavily with icing sugar.

Apricot Ice Cream under a Caramel Cage

Caramel is a favourite with confectioners because of its decorative possibilities. It is used here to create a cage to cover a tea-scented apricot ice cream.

Serves 6–8

INGREDIENTS
450 g/1 lb dried apricots
900 ml/1½ pints/3¾ cups cold
  Earl Grey tea
115 g/4 oz/¾ cup soft light
  brown sugar
30 ml/2 tbsp brandy or gin
  (optional)
300 ml/½ pint/1¼ cups whipping
  cream

FOR THE DECORATION
500 g/1¼ lb/2½ cups caster
  sugar
175 ml/6 fl oz/¾ cup water
120 ml/4 fl oz/½ cup liquid
  glucose
oil, for greasing

*soft light
brown sugar*

caster sugar

brandy

*Earl Grey
tea bags*

*liquid
glucose*

*dried
apricots*

whipping cream

1 Place the apricots in a large bowl, Pour the cold Earl Grey tea over, cover and soak for 4 hours or overnight.

4 Whip the cream in a large bowl until soft peaks form. Fold in the apricot purée and mix well. Transfer to a container suitable for freezing and freeze for 2 hours. Beat with an electric mixer until smooth, then return to the freezer for at least 8 hours. Or, place in an ice cream maker and freeze according to the manufacturer's instructions.

2 Tip the apricots and the tea into a saucepan. Add the brown sugar. Bring to the boil, stirring to dissolve the sugar. Simmer gently for 15–20 minutes until the apricots are tender. Allow to cool.

5 Meanwhile, make the decoration. Place the sugar and water in a small saucepan. Heat gently, stirring until the sugar dissolves. Bring to the boil and add the liquid glucose. Cook until the mixture is a pale caramel. Cool slightly. Lightly oil the back of a ladle.

3 Process the apricots with the cooking liquid in a food processor to a rough purée; the apricots should be chopped but still identifiable. Stir in the brandy or gin, if using.

6 Using a teaspoon, trail caramel over the ladle in horizontal and vertical lines, until a "cage" is built. Leave to harden then gently ease off. Repeat with the remaining caramel, reheating if necessary, to make 6–8 "cages". To serve, set a cage over scoops of ice cream.

Chocolate Grapevine with Chocolate Leaves

Few people can resist a chocolate truffle and this provides a perfect chance to show off with home-made truffles made to look like a bunch of grapes, with chocolate branches and leaves.

Makes 30–40 truffles

INGREDIENTS
450 g/1 lb plain chocolate, chopped
50 g/2 oz/¼ cup butter
175 ml/6 fl oz/¾ cup double cream
450 g/1 lb milk chocolate

FOR THE DECORATION
115 g/4 oz plain chocolate, melted
oil, for brushing
4 rose leaves, washed and dried

milk chocolate

plain chocolate

butter

double cream

COOK'S TIP
Leaves that are nicely shaped and shiny, with well-defined veins, make the best chocolate leaves. Holly works well, as do rose leaves, but avoid any poisonous leaves.

1 Melt the plain chocolate and butter in a bowl set over a pan of hot water. Place the cream in a second bowl and whisk until firm peaks form. Fold the cream into the chocolate mixture, cover and chill for 4–5 hours until firm.

2 Using a melon baller dipped in hot water, scoop the chocolate mixture into balls. Place on a sheet of greaseproof paper.

3 Grate half the milk chocolate on to a sheet of greaseproof paper; melt the remainder. Dip each truffle in melted chocolate then roll in grated chocolate. Allow to set. Arrange the truffles on a dish to resemble a bunch of grapes.

4 Make the decoration. Use a little melted dark chocolate to pipe a "Y" on to greaseproof paper. Chill until set. Peel off the paper gently and place the "Y" at the top of the bunch of truffles.

5 Very lightly oil the leaves, then brush them with the remaining melted dark chocolate to make a coating at least 3 mm/⅛ in thick. Chill until set.

6 Carefully peel the real leaves away from the chocolate. Using a tiny dot of melted chocolate, stick the chocolate leaves to the branch.

Fruits, Cakes and Bakes

Poached Figs with Mascarpone Quenelles

Quenelles are an edible garnish – here they are made of mascarpone, but they can be formed in the same way with other creamy-textured foods such as meringue, ice cream or sorbet.

Serves 6

INGREDIENTS
18 fresh figs
350 ml/12 fl oz/1½ cups red
  wine
115 g/4 oz/½ cup caster sugar
3 strips of orange rind

FOR THE QUENELLES
275 g/10 oz/1¼ cups
  mascarpone cheese
90 g/3½ oz/scant ½ cup fromage
  frais
30–45 ml/2–3 tbsp icing sugar,
  sifted
30 ml/2 tbsp Madeira

orange

icing sugar

caster sugar

red wine

Madeira

mascarpone cheese

figs

fromage frais

1 Place the figs in a saucepan with the red wine, caster sugar and orange rind. Bring to the boil, then simmer for 5–10 minutes until tender. Using a slotted spoon, transfer the figs to a bowl. Bring the red wine syrup back to the boil and cook until reduced by half. Cool slightly.

2 Make the quenelles. Beat together the mascarpone cheese and fromage frais. Sift over the icing sugar, add the Madeira and stir to combine.

3 Take two large metal spoons. Scoop up a spoonful of the mascarpone mixture and invert the second spoon on top of it. Push down and scoop the mixture on to the second spoon.

4 Invert the first spoon a third of the way over the mixture, push down and scoop as before. This will create an oval wedge. Repeat this action to create an oval with three sides. Ease gently off the spoon and place on individual plates next to the warm figs, with a little syrup spooned around.

Lacy Chocolate Soufflés

A dusting of icing sugar sets off many desserts and cakes. For a special effect, dust through a doily to create a perfect pattern.

Serves 6

INGREDIENTS
175 g/6 oz plain chocolate,
  chopped
150 g/5 oz/¾ cup unsalted
  butter, plus extra for greasing
4 eggs, separated
30 ml/2 tbsp whisky
50 g/2 oz/¼ cup caster sugar
icing sugar, for dusting

eggs   *caster sugar*

butter

icing sugar

plain chocolate   *whisky*

1 Preheat the oven to 220°C/425°F/
Gas 7. Grease 6 ramekins. Melt the
chocolate and butter in heatproof bowl
over hot but not boiling water. Allow to
cool slightly, then beat in the egg yolks
and whisky.

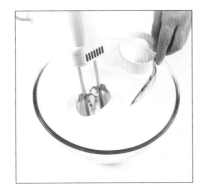

2 Whisk the egg whites in a large
grease-free bowl until soft peaks form.
Gradually add the caster sugar, a
spoonful at a time, continuing to whisk
constantly until the mixture is stiff and
glossy. Beat a third of the whites into
the chocolate mixture to lighten it, then
fold in the rest.

COOK'S TIP
To create a pattern on the plate
too, first lay the doily on the
plate and dust with icing sugar.
Lift off the doily, then place the
decorated soufflé on top.

3 Spoon carefully into the prepared
ramekins, place on a baking sheet,
transfer to the oven and bake for about
10 minutes until well risen. Put on to
individual plates.

4 Hold a doily over a soufflé, then sift
icing sugar generously through the doily
so that both the soufflé and plate are
dusted. Quickly repeat with the other
soufflés. Serve immediately.

Poached Pears with Cinnamon Stacks

Stacks of cinnamon sticks make an attractive addition to a plate – simply tie them together with gold ribbon.

Serves 6

INGREDIENTS
6 eating pears
750 ml/1¼ pints/3 cups ruby port
105 ml/7 tbsp caster sugar
2 cinnamon sticks

FOR THE DECORATION
36 cinnamon sticks
6 gold ribbons, each 30 cm/ 12 in long

ruby port

caster sugar

cinnamon sticks

pears

gold ribbons

1 Peel the pears, leaving the stalks intact. Push the end of a swivel-blade vegetable peeler into the base of each pear to a depth of about 4 cm/1½ in. Twist and remove the core.

2 Slice 5 mm/¼ in off the bottom of each pear so that it will stand upright. Stand the pears in a saucepan that will hold them comfortably but snugly. Add the port, sugar and cinnamon sticks.

3 Bring the port to the boil, cover, lower the heat and simmer for about 15–20 minutes until the pears are tender. Transfer the pears to a dish and keep hot. Boil the port syrup until reduced by half.

4 Meanwhile, make the decoration. Gather the cinnamon sticks together in bundles of six.

5 Tie a length of ribbon around the centre of each bundle. Finish in a bow and trim the ends of the ribbons into a point. Stand the pears in individual bowls, pour a little of the port syrup over and decorate the rim of each bowl with a stack of cinnamon sticks.

COOK'S TIP
Try to use long cinnamon sticks for this garnish – they look far more attractive than shorter ones. Look out for them in delicatessens and Oriental stores.

Pavlova Roulade with Cream Swirls

Soft swirls of cream and strawberries make a pretty decoration for this meltingly light meringue.

Serves 8–10

INGREDIENTS
5 ml/1 tsp vanilla essence
5 ml/1 tsp cornflour
5 ml/1 tsp white wine vinegar
5 egg whites
300 g/11 oz/scant 1½ cups caster sugar
400 ml/14 fl oz/1⅔ cups double cream
150 g/5 oz/¾ cup fromage frais
45 ml/3 tbsp icing sugar, sifted
15 ml/1 tbsp lemon juice
30 ml/2 tbsp grated lemon rind
175 g/6 oz strawberries, thinly sliced

FOR THE DECORATION
75 g/3 oz strawberries
120 ml/4 fl oz/½ cup double cream
icing sugar, for dusting

icing sugar

white wine vinegar

double cream

caster sugar

vanilla essence

strawberries

fromage frais

eggs

lemon

1 Preheat the oven to 150°C/300°F/Gas 2. Line the base and sides of a 33 x 23 cm/13 x 9 in Swiss roll tin with non-stick baking paper. Mix the vanilla essence, cornflour and vinegar in a small bowl and set aside.

2 Whisk the egg whites until soft peaks form. Add the caster sugar, a spoonful at a time, whisking constantly until the mixture is stiff and glossy. Whisk in the cornflour mixture before adding the final spoonful of sugar. Spoon into the tin and spread over evenly. Bake for 25 minutes.

3 Dust a sheet of greaseproof paper with icing sugar. Invert the meringue on to the paper, peel off the lining paper, cover lightly and cool. Whip the cream until soft peaks form. Fold in the fromage frais, icing sugar, lemon juice and rind and spread over the meringue to within 1 cm/½ in of the edges.

4 Sprinkle the sliced strawberries evenly over the cream. Then, using the greaseproof paper underneath as a guide, roll the meringue up from one long edge. Carefully transfer to a serving plate and dust with icing sugar.

5 To decorate, cut the strawberries in half lengthways, then into quarters, leaving on any leaves. Whip the cream and spoon it into a piping bag fitted with a star nozzle.

6 Pipe swirls of cream at intervals along the top of the roulade – these can be used as portion guides. Top each swirl with a strawberry quarter. Dust each serving with icing sugar, if liked, and serve.

Lemon and Lime Tart with Caramelized Citrus Rind

Add a tangy touch with this crunchy decoration.

Serves 8–10

INGREDIENTS
50 g/2 oz/¼ cup caster sugar
40 g/1½ oz/¾ cup ground
   almonds
165 g/5½ oz/scant 1½ cups
   plain flour
130 g/4½ oz/scant ½ cup butter,
   cubed
1 egg, beaten
15 ml/1 tbsp cold water

FOR THE FILLING
8 egg yolks
350 g/12 oz/1½ cups caster
   sugar
300 ml/½ pint/1¼ cups double
   cream
grated rind and juice of
   2 lemons
grated rind and juice of 2 limes

FOR THE DECORATION
2 lemons
2 limes
30–45 ml/2–3 tbsp icing sugar

lemons
icing sugar
butter
limes
ground almonds
eggs
plain flour
caster sugar
double cream

1 Preheat the oven to 180°C/350°F/ Gas 4. Place the sugar, ground almonds and flour in a food processor and process briefly to mix. Add the butter and process until the mixture resembles coarse breadcrumbs. Add the egg and process for just long enough to bind the ingredients, adding the water if necessary. Knead lightly on a floured surface, then roll out to a round large enough to line a deep 25 cm/10 in tart tin.

2 Flip the pastry over the rolling pin, lift it up over the tin and gently ease in. Prick the base, line with non-stick baking paper and fill with baking beans. Bake blind for 15 minutes, then remove the beans and paper and return the pastry case to the oven for 5 minutes more. Allow to cool slightly. Lower the oven temperature to 150°C/300°F/Gas 2.

3 Meanwhile make the filling. Whisk the egg yolks and sugar together in a large bowl. Pour the cream and citrus juices over and whisk in, then fold in both lots of rind. Pour into the pastry case and bake for 45–50 minutes until set. Allow to cool completely.

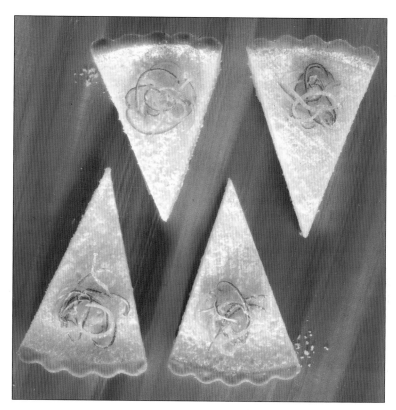

4 Make the decoration. Using a swivel-blade peeler, remove the rind from the lemons and limes in long strips. Slice into fine julienne. Place in a small saucepan of water, bring to the boil, then simmer for 5 minutes. Drain, refresh under cold water and drain again. Pat dry with kitchen paper.

5 Spread out the rind on a sheet of greaseproof paper and dredge with icing sugar. Toss to coat, then tip on to a foil-lined grill pan. Grill for 2–3 minutes until the sugar just melts. Leave to cool and harden. Pile the caramelized rind on top of the citrus tart, dust with more icing sugar and serve.

Spiced Mango Filo Fingers

Mangoes have a wonderful texture and look great simply sliced and fanned out next to these crunchy filo fingers.

Serves 8–10

INGREDIENTS
4 mangoes
6 filo pastry sheets
90 g/3½ oz/7 tbsp butter, melted
45 g/3 tbsp soft light brown sugar
20 ml/4 tsp ground cinnamon
icing sugar, for dusting

soft light brown sugar

butter

filo pastry

mangoes

ground cinnamon

1 Preheat the oven to 200°C/400°F/ Gas 6. Set the most perfect mango aside for the decoration. Peel the remaining mangoes and slice the flesh from either side of the stone. Cut the flesh across into 3 mm/⅛ in thick slices.

2 Keeping the rest of the filo covered with a damp dish towel, lay one sheet on a baking sheet and brush with melted butter. Mix the brown sugar and cinnamon together in a small bowl and sprinkle one-fifth of the mixture over the filo. Lay another sheet of filo on top and repeat. Reserving a little butter, continue layering in this way and end with a filo sheet.

3 Brush the top filo sheet with butter, trim off the excess pastry and lay the sliced mango in neat rows across the layered filo, to cover it completely. Brush with the reserved butter and bake for 30 minutes. Allow to cool, then cut into fingers.

4 Slice the flesh from either side of the stone of the reserved mango. Cut each piece in half lengthways. Make five long cuts, almost to the end, in each quarter. Dust with icing sugar. Put on a plate and fan out the slices. Serve with the mango fingers.

Blackberry and Apple Pie with a Pastry Rose

Pastry is perfect for shaping; here roses and leaves are used to decorate a special fruit pie.

Serves 8–10

INGREDIENTS
250 g/9 oz/2¼ cups plain flour
50 g/2 oz/½ cup icing sugar,
  sifted
200 g/7 oz/scant 1 cup unsalted
  butter, diced
1 egg yolk
15–30 ml/1–2 tbsp cold water
beaten egg, for glazing

FOR THE FILLING
450 g/1 lb cooking apples
30 ml/2 tbsp water
450 g/1 lb blackberries
45 ml/3 tbsp crème de cassis
sugar, to taste

cooking apples

plain flour

blackberries

icing sugar

butter

egg

crème de casssis

1 Preheat the oven to 190°C/375°F/ Gas 5. Place the flour, icing sugar and butter in a food processor and process until the mixture resembles coarse breadcrumbs. Add the egg yolk and enough water to bind the dough. Process for 5–10 seconds. Knead lightly on a floured surface. Wrap and chill.

2 Quarter, peel, core and chop the apples. Place in a saucepan with the water, cover and cook over a low heat until cooked to a fluffy pulp. Add the blackberries and cook for 5 minutes more, then stir in the cassis and sugar to taste. Remove from the heat.

3 Pinch off one-sixth of the pastry and set it aside. Divide the rest in half. Roll out one piece to a large round and use to line a deep 20 cm/8 in pie dish. Spoon in the blackberry and apple mixture, then roll out a lid from the second large piece of pastry and cover the filling. Crimp the edges of the pie.

4 Roll out the remaining pastry thinly. Cut two strips, one 10 x 2 cm/4 x ¾ in, and the other 13 x 2.5 cm/5 x 1 in. Loosely roll up each strip, pinching together occasionally. Pinch the bases and shape into roses.

5 Cut two 13 cm x 5 mm/5 x ¼ in strips for stems. Cut 5 cm/2 in leaf shapes out of the remaining pastry and mark on veins with a sharp knife.

6 Brush the pie with a little water and arrange the roses, stems and leaves on top. Brush the pastry lid and decoration with beaten egg. Bake for 30 minutes until golden. Serve hot or cold.

Chocolate Almond Cake
with Chocolate-dipped Fruit

Chocolate-dipped physalis and strawberries create a
perfect partnership for this gorgeous chocolate cake.

Serves 8–10

INGREDIENTS

250 g/9 oz plain chocolate,
  chopped
115 g/4 oz/½ cup butter, plus
  extra for greasing
4 size 2 eggs, separated
130 g/4½ oz/scant ½ cup caster
  sugar
115 g/4 oz/1 cup ground
  almonds
60 ml/4 tbsp brandy, rum
  or Madeira

FOR THE DECORATION

8 physalis
50 g/2 oz plain chocolate,
  melted
8 strawberries
cocoa powder, for dusting

plain chocolate

ground almonds

eggs

caster sugar

brandy

butter

strawberries

physalis

1 Preheat the oven to 180°C/350°F/
Gas 4. Grease and line the base of a
shallow 25 cm/10 in round cake tin.
Melt the chocolate and butter together
in a large heatproof bowl. In a separate
bowl, whisk the egg yolks with half of
the sugar until thick and pale.

2 Whisk the egg yolks into the
chocolate mixture. Fold in the ground
almonds and brandy, rum or Madeira.

3 Whisk the egg whites in a large
grease-free bowl until soft peaks form.
Gradually add the remaining sugar, a
spoonful at a time, continuing to whisk
constantly until the mixture is stiff and
glossy. Beat one-third into the chocolate
mixture, then fold in the rest.

4 Pour into the tin and tap it sharply
on the work surface to remove any air
bubbles. Bake for 40 minutes or until a
fine skewer inserted in the cake comes
out clean. Invert on to a cake board or
plate, placed on a wire rack. Allow to
cool – the cake should sink slightly.

5 Make the decoration. Tear open the
papery husks of the physalis and twist
back to form a little umbrella. Have
ready a sheet of non-stick baking paper
on a baking sheet.

6 Holding a physalis by the husks,
half-dip the fruit in the melted
chocolate. Put on the non-stick baking
paper to set. Repeat with all the
strawberries. Dust the cake with cocoa.
Serve the cake decorated with the
dipped fruit.

Crêpes with Oranges and Meringue Crests

Meringue crests appear as perfect pinnacles on top of delicate crêpes filled with tangy oranges.

Serves 6–8

INGREDIENTS
115 g/4 oz/1 cup plain flour
15 ml/1 tbsp caster sugar
pinch of salt
1 egg
300 ml/½ pint/1¼ cups milk
50 g/2 oz/¼ cup butter, melted
oil, for frying

FOR THE FILLING
50 g/2 oz/¼ cup butter
4 oranges
50 g/2 oz/½ cup icing sugar,
  sifted
30 ml/2 tbsp Cointreau or other
  orange-flavoured liqueur

FOR THE DECORATION
2 egg whites
50 g/2 oz/¼ cup caster sugar

caster sugar

plain flour

oranges

milk

egg *butter*

Cointreau

icing sugar

1 Preheat the oven to 200°C/400°F/ Gas 6. Sift the flour, sugar and salt into a mixing bowl. Beat the egg into the milk in a jug or bowl, then gradually whisk into the flour to form a smooth batter. Whisk in the melted butter.

2 Heat a little oil in a small frying pan. Pour in a thin layer of batter, tilting to coat the pan. Cook for 20–25 seconds until golden underneath. Flip over and cook for 10–15 seconds. Make more crêpes in the same way.

3 Wipe the pan with kitchen paper and melt the butter. When it starts to bubble, add the orange segments and icing sugar. Cook for 5 minutes, stirring occasionally. Add the liqueur and warm through. Remove and keep warm.

4 Pare the rind from one of the oranges into fine strips using a zester. Peel and segment the oranges. Set aside. Whisk the egg whites until soft peaks form. Gradually add the sugar, a spoonful at a time, whisking constantly until stiff and glossy. Spoon into a piping bag fitted with a star nozzle.

5 Make the decoration. Line a baking sheet with non-stick baking paper. Fold a crêpe in half. Spoon several orange segments and a little sauce on one half, then fold over to make a triangular shape enclosing the filling. Place on the prepared baking sheet. Fill the remaining crêpes in the same way.

6 Pipe a row of meringue shells down the centre of each pancake triangle. Bake for 5–6 minutes until the meringue is golden. Serve at once with the remaining sauce, decorated with the orange rind.

INDEX